Volume one, 1964

A Repertory Theater Publication
in association with Playbill, Inc.

THEATRE

*The Annual of the Repertory Theater
of Lincoln Center*

Barry Hyams, *Editor*

Contents

Introduction

The Common Sense of Insanity
by S. N. Behrman

BROOKS ATKINSON once said to me of Robert Whitehead that he was not only one of the most sensitive of Broadway producers, but also a poet. I decided to overlook these defects and gave him my new play which I hoped he would produce in one of the Broadway theatres he controls. Mr. Whitehead gave the play to Mr. Kazan who consented to direct it, and I felt all set for another spin of the Broadway roulette wheel. My first spin had been in 1927 with the Theatre Guild and the Lunts. I have been spinning ever since and by this time had become a hardened gambler. Though I had never hit the jackpot, I had had enough varying success in the span of thirty-six years to keep off the relief rolls. Mr. Whitehead had already produced one play of mine. I had to do considerable rewriting on the road before the Broadway opening and in that tremulous period the poetic blemish about which Mr. Atkinson had warned me proved to be a creative asset. The Broadway opening of my new play suffered a delay at the very start because Mr. Kazan, after reading and accepting it, had to go to Athens for the filming of *America America*. By this time also, Mr. Whitehead and Mr. Kazan were involved in their burgeoning plans for the Repertory Theater of Lincoln Center. They were to open the 1963–1964 season at the Vivian Beaumont Theater in Lincoln Square. It is one among the cluster of temples of art in various stages of growth there. Mr. Kazan, on one of his brief commuting trips from Athens to New York, suggested to me that my play would be suitable for the Lincoln Center project. I had seen a model of the projected theatre in Mr. Whitehead's office, and it is enchanting. The idea of having a play of mine in it was tantalizing, but then it appeared that the funds for the completion of the theatre would not be available for the '63 season. That daydream vanished and Mr. Whitehead and I tried to figure out when the Broadway production of my play could open, since it would have to wait until Mr. Kazan was through with the cutting of his film.

I had lunch with Mr. Whitehead one day in the tiny La Strada restaurant on 46th Street. The poetic lesion from which he suffers is never apparent except when he is discussing creatively the meaning of a play in relationship to the life we know and have to put up with. Otherwise, you might easily mistake him for a practical man of affairs. He began to tell me about a plan he had, pending the completion of the Vivian Beaumont Theater, to put up a *temporary* theatre on ground offered him for one dollar a year by the Regents of New York University. He began to sketch this theatre—a "steel tent," he called it— on the back of the La Strada menu. I listened, incredulous.
    "What will you do with the temporary theatre when the Vivian Beaumont is ready?" I asked him.
    "Demolish it," he said.
    I found myself remembering hazily the medieval notion that poets were insane. The idea of building a theatre with the sole object of demolishing it, seemed to me, to put it charitably, bizarre. I know that there are notorious and widely applauded contemporary artists who create elaborate constructs in order to demolish them; but then, these constructs are made of old automobile tires, fenders, nuts, bolts, discarded pianos picked up in junk yards, so that their demolition only restores the ingredients to their original condition. But you can't pick up a theatre in a junk yard! I began to think of a psychiatrist friend of mine who might possibly help Mr. Whitehead. But I did not express my fear to him; I only made a mild inquiry about the economics of building theatres for demolition. Mr. Whitehead then switched from art to economics; he stopped drawing the doomed theatre and began putting down figures. He said that the cost of the structure would be less than the rental of a Broadway theatre for a year and a half. He knew about this because he had, for example, paid rent for a Broadway theatre during the run of *A Man For All Seasons*.

The structure would cost less than the price of one of those ephemeral, astronomically expensive pre-sold musicals that, once they are revealed, do not sell.

Going uptown in the taxi after lunch, I comforted myself with the thought that this chimera would never materialize and that when I saw Mr. Whitehead again, he would have forgotten it. I hoped that he would again be what we loosely describe as "normal" and that we could go ahead with planning for the Broadway production of my play. I trusted that Mr. Whitehead would get better without the intervention of my psychiatrist friend, but he didn't. He persisted in his fantasy so that it became a fixation. Months passed. Mr. Whitehead became so involved with civic authorities whom he had to convince that the proposed theatre would not violate the fire laws, with architects, contractors, and politicians and bankers, that I saw very little of him, and all this time Mr. Kazan was away in Athens. Then one night in the following May I ran into Mr. Kazan somewhat unexpectedly in the East Room of the White House. It was a great state dinner for the French Minister of Culture, André Malraux. Lounging about, sipping champagne in the East Room, waiting for the receiving line to form, I saw Julie Harris, Tennessee Williams, Arthur Miller, Saul Bellow, Leonard Bernstein, Edmund Wilson, Irwin Shaw, Thornton Wilder, Robert Penn Warren, Paddy Chayefsky and Elia Kazan. It was a cross between Sardi's and a meeting of the Authors' League. Kazan came up to me: "Why don't you give up the idea of a Broadway production," he said, "and save your play for Lincoln Center?" I don't know whether it was the general excitement of the evening, the anticipation of presently meeting the President and the First Lady, or Mr. Kazan's ignescent personality that made me suddenly feel that this was the only destiny for my play and for me. I said "yes." It was probably the first theatrical deal ever consummated in the White House. We shook hands on it just as some Marines, bearing great Presidential standards, marched through the main center doors of the East Room to a blare of trumpets and a voice announcing: "The President of the United States." The spectacle was thrilling. It was Shakespearean. It was like *Henry the Fifth*.

Later that summer, in July, I went down to Fourth Street for the ground-breaking ceremonies for the "steel tent." On an improvised wooden platform in the middle of a corrugated and somewhat muddy lot, Mr. Paul Screvane, on behalf of the Mayor who was out of town, Mr. Robert Dowling, Peggy Wood and Chancellor Stoddard of the University made welcoming remarks. When these were over, a great crane, bearing a sizeable bucket, made a slow swoop downwards and scooped up a chunk of earth. At that moment I caught a glimpse of Mr. Whitehead's face. It was flushed and I thought I saw in his eyes the fanatic's vision of a better world. As we walked over to Chancellor Stoddard's house, where we were to be regaled with champagne, I spoke of this to Mr. Kazan. "I noticed it too," he said; "it is Bob's day. He has lived for this day!" Through the rest of the summer and fall I saw Mr. Whitehead only occasionally and Mr. Kazan not at all. I often sat in my room wondering whether a second scoop of earth had ever been removed. I thought it quite possible that the workmen, in a fit of absent-mindedness, had gone on to more durable projects.

"We are almost on schedule," was Whitehead's invariable report when I spoke to him on the telephone. Mostly, it was impossible to get him. He was always at "the site." I went on to other projects, thinking occasionally of that untilled, lonely lot on Fourth Street. One night in October I was summoned to Mr. Whitehead's office to meet the Lincoln Center acting company. Many of the artists I knew. Whitehead, Kazan, Arthur Miller, José Quintero and Harold Clurman addressed them. Though unrecorded, they were memorable and moving speeches. Mr. Whitehead said that the Center hoped to do a wide variety of plays, past and contemporary, that he hoped that all of them would have, ultimately, a common reference to the possibility of a more civilized and humane life in this country. Mr. Kazan spoke very movingly of his friend, Clifford Odets, who had died in exile and unfulfilled, several weeks before. "Had such a project as this existed during his creative years," Kazan said, "Odets might have died at home, spiritually speaking, instead of in exile." Kazan warned the company about the difficulties they and himself would encounter. He had no idea, for instance, how he would put on Mr. Miller's unusually complicated play, but he hoped that he and they would find a way. Mr. Quintero made a very funny speech in which he expressed,

with Latin gusto, his enlistment in this adventure because, he shouted,
"In the theatre I like excitement!" His speech generated excitement
as he was delivering it. Mr. Clurman, with an apoplectic fervor—
appropriate for the author of *The Fervent Years*, a superb record of
the history of the Group Theatre in which he, Lee Strasberg, Kazan
and Odets were involved—contrasted the eager response which the
public had already evidenced toward the Lincoln Center repertory
company with the bleak and meager resources of the Group Theatre.
He told the company of actors that they were lucky.

When I got home that night I felt lucky myself, at an advanced
age, to be in at the birth of a revolutionary adventure made possible
by the energies and creative enthusiasm of younger men.

Early in January 1964, I returned to the lonely lot on Fourth Street
to see a rehearsal of Arthur Miller's play. The scoop made by the first
shovel in July had widened and deepened; there was a theatre in the
cavity! I walked into it. It took my breath away. It is, as Mr. Kazan
says, "a knockout."

"It is a good theatre," Mr. Clurman says, "because the moment
you enter it, your attention is riveted on the stage." Mine was and on
Mr. Mielziner's fascinatingly patterned design for Mr. Miller's play.
The theatre is there. It exists. It is unadorned and beautiful with the
spare beauty of the functional. It is inconceivable that a theatre such
as this will be demolished. It is the only one of Mr. Whitehead's plans
which will, I am sure, miscarry. He thought he was building a temporary theatre. (But perhaps Mr. Whitehead always had an arriére-
pensée about this!) He has built a permanent one which will add im-
measurably to the cultural life of this city. There should be theatres
like this in every borough. I have felt for a great many years, together
with lots of other people, that the regional theatre is the only hope
for a living theatre in this country. I hope that the sprouting regional
movement will infiltrate the vast community of New York, and that
the various segments of it will have their own theatre with Mr. Whitehead's "temporary theatre" as its prototype. I have often wondered
why every German city has five or six independent theatres. Of
course, they are all subsidized. I have tried to explain to myself why
it is considered natural for the various arts in this country (museums,

concert halls, opera, etc.) to be subsidized, but that it is considered abnormal to subsidize a theatre. I think the reason is historical and certainly no longer valid. The fact is that when I started writing plays, the theatre was indeed a flourishing institution in New York and on the road. It made money, and when you are affluent, you cannot reasonably ask for a hand-out. But since then the theatre has been swallowed up by the cannibalism of the mechanical arts. It is no longer self-supporting. People have always expected music and art not to pay. They have to learn to credit us with the same gift of insolvency. The other arts are traditional, and therefore cherished, indigents. But I think we now can lay claim to belong to this honorable company. We are indigent too and can unashamedly plead for subsidy.

In 1949 I was in England and received an invitation to go to Frankfurt, Germany, to have a look at the theatres there. England was still suffering from the effects of the war. When I complained in various hotels about the cold rooms, the hall porter usually said to me, with ironic poignance: "Well, you know we won the war!" Well, Germany had lost the war but Frankfurt was busy, well-heated and glutted with food. Also it was glutted with theatres. The General Director of Theatres in German cities is called the Intendant, and the one in Frankfurt took me around on a bleak Sunday in February to have a look at his exhibits. There were five theatres in full swing, large and small, and all packed. The Intendant started me off at the newly completed Frankfurt Opera House. I think this is the most magnificently equipped theatre I have ever seen. My guide showed me with pride the mechanism for the revolving stages and the palatial dressing rooms. He took me into the "Director's Box" out front and demonstrated the telephonic devices from it to the conductor, the stage manager, the electrician. I looked around at the vast auditorium. "How did you manage to build this?" I asked. The Intendant laughed. "Marshall Plan," he said briefly.

On the evening I have described in Mr. Whitehead's office, Mr. Kazan told us of Mr. Whitehead's difficulties on the financial side of the Lincoln Center project. "How can you persuade even the most public-spirited of bankers—when you know that even if you sell out, you will have a considerable deficit—not to raise the prices? The persuasion was accomplished," Mr. Kazan went on to say, "and the prices have been kept low in spite of the demand." In Frankfurt, I wondered, perhaps naïvely, how the United States Government saw its way clear to subsidizing the German theatres but could do nothing for ours. Thanks to President and Mrs. Kennedy's interest in the arts, there has come to be a new attitude about this. It is generally recognized that the so-called commercial Broadway theatre is in crisis. There is something eternally refreshing in the human spirit. When crisis hardens into the rigidity of impasse, this spirit revives. It refuses to be choked. It is resilient. It becomes fertile with ingenuity. It blossoms into vista.

"We did not set out to design an open stage . . . it evolved." Robert
Whitehead in foreground; left to right, Arthur Miller, Elia Kazan,
Jo Mielziner.

A Famous Repertory Theatre
by *Alfred Harbage*

THE FIRST TIME I heard Shakespeare praised by anyone but my father was in a Chautauqua tent in Bucks County when it was still a rural community visited by cultural missionaries. The speaker loved his subject, and his words were truly moving. It was without resentment that I later learned that most of his facts were wrong. He pictured the actors for whom Shakespeare wrote as a rout of beggarly strollers, barnstorming in the provinces when they were not sharking upon riffraff audiences in a primitive London. In the circumstances, he said, the poetic drama of the Bard must be viewed as a flower that bloomed on a dunghill—a literary *miracle*.

But even though he was born four centuries ago, Shakespeare lived this side the age of miracles. If his actors had been what the speaker described (as once commonly supposed), his plays would not be what they are; in fact they would not exist. Actually they were plays of quality presented by a company of quality, stable in character, superior in artistry and wonderfully canny in its working methods. It established touch with an audience of quality. This company deserves a moment of contemplation by anyone interested in the repertory movement today, not as a thing to be imitated, but as a source of inspiration.

Since it was called "The Lord Chamberlain's Men (or Servants)" in Queen Elizabeth's reign, and "The King's Men (or Servants)" in King James's reign, it is sometimes pictured in a way opposite to that of the Chautauqua lecturer; in fact, as a nest of "kept" entertainers nurtured in a noble or royal household, like an orchestra of the Hapsburgs, catering to the courtly except when it deigned to give a few public performances. Of course it was not like that at all. A company was obliged to obtain a nominal patron in order to have legal identity, since there was no craft guild for actors, but this patron gave little except his name, a license, and a badge—no substantial form of subsidy. An Elizabethan theatrical company was on its own, its only true patrons the people of England who paid to see it perform.

There had been religious drama in England, non-professionally acted, for five centuries before Shakespeare's time. There had been secular drama in England, professionally acted, for over a century before Shakespeare's time. But the early professional troupes were small clusters of manor-house servants or itinerants, resembling minstrel bands, and the pieces they offered were rudimentary "interludes." The upsurge in the quality of the drama came when the acting fraternity achieved a fair degree of affluence and could afford to enlist literary talent. The single event most influential in creating the needed affluence was the building (on borrowed money) of a regular theatre in the London area by the actor James Burbage in 1576 when Shakespeare was twelve years old. Previously the only English "theatres" had been any halls, inns, plots of ground, or barrel-and-board stages where the actors could find room to act.

A second public theatre was built in the area the year after the first, and eight additional ones by 1616, the year of Shakespeare's death. Theatres fell into disuse because of competition and dilapidation so that rarely were more than three operating at one time, but in view of the fact that each had a capacity of several thousand, and the total population of the London area was less than two hundred thousand, their number is imposing enough. In two decades the city had become the most "theatrical" metropolis in the world.

The theatres were the body not the soul of the enterprise. The soul was the acting companies and their repertories in a new liaison with the public which the theatres were making possible. The companies did not own the theatres but rented them, and a company might shift from one to another without loss of clientele or sense of direction. The rental was a fixed proportion of gate receipts. Naturally the owners preferred to rent to companies which could cohere, survive and attract large audiences since the rental income would be proportionately large. The cost of the theatres (high) is known in most cases, and the rental yield (amazingly high) in several. The approximate income of the actor-tenants (substantial) is also known, but it would be pointless, or even tactless, to parade the hard facts here.

We do not know whether Shakespeare was a company member or a hired actor during the first half dozen years of his career. In 1592 he was alluded to as "excellent in the quality he professes." Since acting was not one of the traditional "crafts" descended from the middle ages, and fitted into no professional category, the search for a term for it had resulted in the gentle ambiguity, "the quality"; hence the allusion means simply that Shakespeare was an excellent actor also known for his "grace in writing." In 1594 he became a member of the newly organized Lord Chamberlain's Men, along with others "excellent in the quality." One was Richard Burbage, son of the first theatre-builder and destined to become the greatest actor of the age. Another was the master of drollery, Will Kempe, who became the original Dogberry. Other charter members were Thomas Pope, John Hemmings, Augustine Phillips and George Bryan. Soon added, if not in the original group, were William Sly and Henry Condell. Here then were the first nine members of perhaps the most remarkable acting troupe of record.

It bore strong witness to a man's natural capacity if he became a company member, more than to be born a lord. There were hundreds of actors in London and on the road, but only a few would ever become actor-sharers in such an organization as the Lord Chamberlain's Men. Drawn together by awareness of superior talent and by mutual trust, they were legally bound by a deed of association. New members could be added by common consent, but normally only to fill vacancies through death or retirement, so that the number would remain about ten. There was nothing starry-eyed about Elizabethans in business, and this was a serious business. The only capital of the group was their own money, their own energies and their own natural gifts. Perhaps Shakespeare's "grace in writing" was more important than his acting ability in winning him his place, but he was probably a good actor. As "actor-sharers" these men would rent a theatre, buy play-scripts and costumes and act all principal roles. They would hire additional actors, as well as musicians, wardrobe-keeper, stage-keeper and prompter. They themselves would be the producer-directors. They would share proceeds after expenses.

The stability of the company is demonstrated in a striking way. In 1616 when Shakespeare died, he left token bequests to the three original members who survived: Burbage, Hemming and Condell. In 1623 only Hemming and Condell remained. These assisted the printers of the Folio collection of the plays, "to keepe the memory of so worthy a Friend & Fellow alive as was our Shakespeare." The volume contains a list of "The Names of the Principall Actors in all these Playes" with a total of twenty-six names, the actor-sharers in the company in the thirty years since 1594. This may be a world's record for small turn-over in a theatrical enterprise. The company, which had been renamed the King's Men in 1603, retained its corporate identity until 1642 when the Civil Wars closed the theatres. The plays of Shakespeare remained a treasure in its repertory.

Before we can properly appraise its role in bringing literature and the public together, we must understand how the company operated. Although only ten actor-sharers comprised the company proper, the whole organization was larger. To use an analogy appropriate in Elizabethan times, the ten were the "master craftsmen." These hired about eight additional actors, younger or less able ones for doubling in minor roles, who may be thought of as "journeymen." As "apprentices," although not so-called, at least half a dozen boys from eight to sixteen years of age would be learning "the quality" and acting the parts of pages or the like, eventually those of the heroines. Each was trained by a particular actor-sharer who often reared the boy in his own home along with his own children. When we add to these actors, large and small, the musicians, fee-gatherers, stage-keeper, wardrobe-keeper, prompter and miscellaneous help, we observe that thirty to forty people would be earning a living in the single theatre occupied by the company. There was no lack of personnel even for Shakespeare's most multi-peopled plays.

On any weekday morning the company would be rehearsing the play next to be added to the repertory. It would probably also be running through the play billed for that particular day. In the afternoon, beginning at two o'clock, it would give its public performance. Then in the evening, if there were no chartered performance at court or elsewhere, the actors would repair to their homes to get the lines for the next play to go into rehearsal. It was a tough regimen, six days of the week for as many as ten months of the year.

There survives an account book kept by a theatre-owner named Philip Henslowe, recording performances in his theatres during several years in the fifteen-nineties. In a long season running from Monday, August 25, 1595, to Friday, July 23, 1596, his Rose Theatre on the Bankside was occupied by the Lord Admiral's Men, at this time the only formidable rivals of Shakespeare's company, which was renting a theatre on the opposite side of town. The company at the Rose acted almost every weekday except for a six-week closing during Lent, a total of two hundred and eighteen performances, presenting thirty-nine different plays, eighteen of them new ones. This means that they were putting on a new play every two weeks, in addition to twenty-one plays surviving in the repertory from former seasons. The same play was never acted on successive days, and rarely in the same week. Even a new play, although attendance was large at openings, would not be billed the next day but would take its place in the repertory, to be offered at widening intervals for the fifteen or so performances for which a play was normally good. This means that there was a constant change in the complexion of the repertory even within a season.

Obviously the company aimed to serve both the resident populace and the constant flux of visitors from the country and abroad, since London was both the capital and a chief port. Anyone visiting the city for two weeks beginning August 25th could have seen at the Rose two new plays, *Longshanks* and *Crack Me This Nut*, and nine different old ones, since there was only one repeat in the twelve playing days. Had he returned for two weeks at the end of the season, he could have seen at this same theatre ten plays he had not seen on his former visit. *Longshanks*, now an "old" play, was the only one that had been billed then, and again there was only one repeat performance in two weeks. On the last day of the season, the company performed *The Tinker of Totness*, a new play! As it is quite a while since anyone has acted in thirty-nine plays in one season, including eighteen "openings," it can be seen why an Elizabethan company must have limited appeal as an object of imitation.

Since we now think of repertory companies, quite properly, as presenting occasional new plays along with "classics" from Shakespeare to Shaw and O'Neill, it may be useful to define what "old" and "new" meant in Shakespeare's time. Although the drama had roots deep in the Middle Ages, the upsurge of secular drama of quality had been so rapid that in 1594 there was only a short "usable" past. The oldest plays performed by the Admiral's Men in the season just reviewed were Christopher Marlowe's *Tamburlain*, *Doctor Faustus* and *The Jew Of Malta*, all less than ten years old in 1595–96. Another play of the vintage of Marlowe's belonging to the Admiral's Men was the very popular *Spanish Tragedy* by Thomas Kyd, but for some reason it was given a rest this season. Such plays were immensely valuable properties, good for many times the fifteen or so performances of the average play. Counterbalancing them were plays that had to be dropped after a few performances because the word-of-mouth publicity was condemnatory; a company had to pocket the loss involved in purchasing the script and rehearsing it. Most of the "old" plays in the repertory were only a year or two old.

Of the new plays fed at such a rapid rate into the repertory by the Admiral's Men this season, only one, George Chapman's *Blind Beggar of Alexandria*, survives. Only six of their "old" ones of the season survive. The figures are typical. It was to a company's advantage to keep its plays out of print. We have scores of titles of Admiral's Men's plays in the years 1594 to 1613 when it was competing with Shakespeare's company, but only thirty actual texts. The unprinted plays represent a great loss. Some of them were written by the gifted poet, Michael Drayton, whose dramatic remains consist now only of a few scenes in a single play. Thomas Heywood was for a time an actor and writer for the company, but four-fifths of his work is lost. Or take the case of Thomas Dekker. In 1599 he wrote for the company the whole of three plays and parts of six others. Could the writing possibly have been any good? It so happens that two of his plays of this year's crop did get into print: one the delightful allegory, *Old Fortunatus*, and the other the golden comedy, *Shoemakers' Holiday*, now included in many anthologies. Dekker was an inspired hack. His earnings from playwriting this year were twice the average annual income of a London mason or shopkeeper—not much perhaps, but a living. The theatres made it possible, for the first time in England, for a man to live by

[6]

creative writing without the aid of a patron. Unluckily for Dekker, he was not also an actor, like Heywood and Shakespeare. Actor-sharers made small fortunes, and theatre-owners large ones. Philip Henslowe and his son-in-law, Edward Alleyn, the Burbage of the Admiral's Men, made enough to endow Dulwich College.

The Admiral's Men were rivals to be reckoned with, possessing as they did the plays of Marlowe and other gifted pioneers and buying new plays from Drayton, Chapman, Dekker, Heywood and a dozen others. Nevertheless, the Chamberlain's Men excelled them, as indicated by the fact that they were more frequently called upon for special performances, and, when James ascended the throne, won the title of the "King's Men" while their rivals became the "Prince's Men." (Order of precedence in a royal family is amusingly illustrated by the fact that the third-runner among the London companies was now re-named the "Queen's Men.") Shakespeare's company won out primarily because he was the most popular writer and Burbage the most popular actor of the era.

We have no account book for the Lord Chamberlain's (King's) Men, but their schedule, six playing days a week through most of the year, would have been like that of the Admiral's (Prince's) Men. Only a few times between 1594 and 1613 did they find it necessary to tour the neighboring shires. Like their rivals, they rented their theatres. Even the Globe, used by them after 1599, was not owned by the company as such, although owned jointly by five of their members, including Shakespeare. Their repertory, except for the prominence in it of Shakespeare's plays, would have resembled that of their rivals, with many new plays fed into it each season. Shakespeare's "hits" would have been good for many times the fifteen or so performances of the usual play, but some of his work simply came and went like that of lesser playwrights. His *Richard the Second* was written about 1595. In 1601 the Essex faction thought it would do them some good if a play was on the boards showing the deposition of a monarch. The Chamberlain's Men, evidently little concerned about the political issue, required a premium of forty shillings to bill *Richard the Second* at the Globe because it was "so old and long out of use that they should have small or no company at it." In a word, this fine play was theatrically obsolete six years after it was written.

[7]

Shakespeare brought with him to the company some of his early work and wrote for it one or usually two plays a year until his retirement. After the turn of the century he seems to have been gradually excused from acting. At a moderate estimate the company brought out ten to fifteen new plays a year by other playwrights most of which were never printed. Luckily the age preserved Shakespeare's work virtually intact. The repertory of his company during his association with it is now represented for us by his thirty-seven plays and by twenty-eight others: five by Ben Jonson, six by Beaumont and Fletcher, one each by Dekker, Chapman and Tourneur and thirteen by miscellaneous playwrights, some of them anonymous. This means that we have, with the thirty extant plays of the chief rival company, a total of ninety-five plays out of at least five hundred which the two companies must have performed between 1594 and 1613.

Judging by the extant plays, the repertory of Shakespeare's company had the edge in quality over that of its chief rival, even with his own plays left out of consideration. Although the seedier plays of his company were just as seedy as the seedier plays of its rival, the percentage of good plays was larger. This tells us something important about the company and why it rose to the top. As good writers appeared on the scene, the company saw that they were good and made a bid for their services. Ben Jonson had been writing journeyman plays at least since 1596, but the first one in which he took pride, *Every Man In His Humour*, was performed by the Chamberlain's Men in 1598 with Burbage and Shakespeare in the cast. In the same way, the company wooed Beaumont and Fletcher from its rivals. This search for quality is something which repertory companies are still free to emulate.

It is true that an Elizabethan company had advantages impossible to recover, quite apart from the stamina of the actors and playwrights for which the word "miraculous" is scarcely too strong. The times themselves were propitious. It was early days in theatrical history, with all the vitality and enthusiasm which such days are apt to bring. There were few competing forms of commercialized entertainment and the London theatres were within reach of the many, not too costly and in walking distance. Furthermore, although the tendency was in that direction, play-going was still not a peculiarly urban activity. There were still plenty of companies and repertories on the road, so that play-going habits were being formed and appetites whetted in various parts of the realm. The drama still had a national audience, and at any performance at the Globe there would be scores of non-Londoners in the audience.

Still it seems to the present writer that some of the old advantages were of an intangible kind, and that the spirit of Shakespeare's company might well be invoked as an aid in shaping our aspirations. The quality above all others which one would like to see reborn in the modern theatre was its sheer generosity. His company wanted to give something to everybody, and the best that it could give. The concrete evidence of the fact is the amazing abundance and variety of its offerings. This might be illustrated by the non-Shakespearean sector of its repertory as well as the Shakespearean, but the reader will be most familiar with the latter. To classify Shakespeare's plays simply as Histories, Comedies, Tragedies, is to give a most misleading impression. The "history," *Richard the Third*, is not in the least like the "history," *Henry the Fourth*, nor is the latter in the least like its successor, *Henry the Fifth*, or its predecessor, *Richard the Second*. So it is with the "comedies" ranging from the broadest farce to the most delicate poetic fantasy, and each different from the others. *Hamlet* and *Antony and Cleopatra* are worlds apart in type although both are "tragedies." Here is not only God's plenty, but God's infinite variety.

Abundance and variety are relative matters, and without trying to match the Elizabethans, a theatrical company today could at least try not to be stingy or narrow. Shakespeare's company strove valiantly not to be narrow. When it ceased billing new history plays, largely because subjects had run out, it kept existent ones in its repertory. At the same time that it staged its mighty *King Lear*, it revived the mild old romance, *Mucedorus*. From 1599 on there was a new kind of competition offered by small coterie theatres staging mainly bitter satirical plays for sophisticated auditors. From some allusions in *Hamlet* we may deduce that Shakespeare took a dim view of their repertories, and yet his company competed occasionally on their terms. It staged one of their plays, Marston's *The Malcontent*, and Shakespeare's own *Troilus and Cressida* may have been intended to woo back sophisticates to the Globe. The company was deferential to changing fashions without becoming enslaved to any fashion.

[9]

In the long run, this is the only way a theatrical company can flourish. The "specialized" companies in Shakespeare's time had short lives. Coteries tend to make thin and fickle audiences. The intelligent general public makes a more reliable one, and the Lord Chamberlain's Men had the advantage of believing in this intelligent general public, as well they might because they were part of it. They were artistic but not arty men, of ordinary breed, evading their taxes only now and then, and sometimes even serving as churchwardens. The important thing is that they were "in touch." A theatre can cease to be "in touch" without quite knowing it, and can cut its own throat simply because suicide is in the air in its immediate vicinity. Sometimes rival forms of entertainment are blamed for eclipsing legitimate drama when the audience of the latter has not been drawn but chased away. If drama becomes repugnant, audiences will shrink not expand; it is as simple as that.

The audience at the Globe sought the ancient values of profit and pleasure. They sought emotional release in laughter and tears, cure for apathy, moral encouragement and a sense of kinship with each other. They did not gather to prove how different they were from others, or how hospitable their minds to the esoteric. They did not view plays as torches lighted one after the other in symbolic defiance of censorship. I hope that the reader will not suspect a Comstockian taint in this discourse if I point to one additional and perhaps surprising fact about the repertories just described. Many of the plays are earthy, totally unsqueamish about sex as about other realities and often peppered with ribald jokes. And yet in all of the ninety-five extant texts one observes a respect for certain proprieties. Obviously actors and audience were in agreement about certain things and self-regulating principles were operating. A search in these plays for those four-letter words which are now often viewed as marks of literary merit will prove quite unrewarding. Play-going was a public and social occasion, and on such occasions people generally were, and still are, embarrassed by overt obscenity and profanity, no matter how sincere. Shakespeare himself has often been "expurgated," but with amazingly little need.

Drama dare not be simply bland and innocuous, and with the Lord Chamberlain's Men it never was. But there is a degree of gaminess which is bound to alienate such "gentles all" as Shakespeare so courteously addressed. These "gentles all" are still around, and perhaps craving a theatre to go to. It is to be hoped that with the spread of the repertory movement, the drama will again be "in touch."

Acknowledgment: Since everything about Shakespeare is assumed to be mysterious, it may seem odd that his company can be discussed in specific terms. Actually much is known about Shakespeare, especially his theatrical milieu, owing not to "discoveries" by this man or that but to the cooperative efforts of literary scholars, some of whom have been superbly gifted as paleographers and sifters of evidence. These men, by their very nature, are unaware that sweet are the uses of publicity, and may work a lifetime without being generally known. The present sketch could not have been written except for the quiet, patient, honest efforts of the late E. K. Chambers and W. W. Greg.

"It is hard to say what effect this theatre will have ... For myself, it would guarantee the continuation of the adventure of playwrighting."
—*Arthur Miller*

Arthur Miller: Theme and Variations
by Harold Clurman

AFTER THE FALL, the opening production of the Repertory Theater of Lincoln Center, is Arthur Miller's first play in nine years. It offers us a vantage point from which to examine the man and his work. It is a bridge from which we may look backward to his starting point and forward to the way ahead.

When recently asked in what way his plays were related to the events of his life Miller replied, "In a sense all my plays are autobiographical." The artist creates his biography through his work even as the events of his life serve to shape him.

He was born on One Hundred Twelfth Street in Manhattan in 1915. He is one of three children. He has an elder brother in business, a sister on the stage. The Millers were unequivocally middle-class and Jewish. His mother, no longer living, was born in the United States; his father, a manufacturer of women's coats, was born in what before the First World War was part of the Austro-Hungarian empire. Till the Depression of the Thirties the Millers were a moderately well-to-do family. Arthur attended grammar school in Harlem and went to high school in Brooklyn.

By the time he finished high school Arthur's parents could no longer afford to send him to college. His grades were not sufficiently high to qualify him for entry into the school of his choice, the University of Michigan. He found two ways out of this dilemma. He got himself a job in a warehouse on Tenth Avenue and Sixtieth Street as a "loader" and shipping clerk. He saved a sum sufficient to pay his tuition. He also wrote a letter to the President of the University and asked for a chance to prove his merit within the first year of his studies. If he failed to distinguish himself he would quit. He did very well and stayed on to take his degree of Bachelor of Arts.

In his boyhood Arthur was neither particularly bright nor very well read. He was a baseball fan. He began to read while working at the warehouse. He is probably the only man who ever read through *War and Peace* entirely on the subway, standing up. At college he also began to write—plays. Several of them were awarded the Jule and Avery Hopwood prize of the University of Michigan. One of them won a prize of $1,250 given by the Theatre Guild's Bureau of New Plays. With money from these prizes and $22.77 a week from the Federal Theatre Project, Miller was able to support himself during the early years of his career. He was living at Patchogue, Long Island, at the time and had to check in every day at the Project office in Manhattan to collect his wage. He wrote a play about Montezuma which was submitted to the Group Theatre, as well as to others, no doubt, and which the author of the present article, then the Group Theatre's Managing Director, found several years later in his files—unread!

In 1944 while visiting various army camps in the United States, a diary Miller kept as research for a film, *The Story of G.I. Joe* (the war life of Ernie Pyle), was published under the title, *Situation Normal*. In 1945, as a reaction to the activities of a Fascist organization known as the Christian Front, Miller wrote his only novel, *Focus*, which attracted considerable attention. Its subject was anti-semitism.

That year saw the production of Miller's first play, *The Man Who Had All The Luck*, which had no luck at all: there were only four performances. Still Miller was launched! One critic, Burton Rascoe, recognized a potentially powerful playwright. More important, several producers including the present writer got in touch with Miller requesting him to submit his next play. That was *All My Sons* which was produced by Harold Clurman, Elia Kazan and Walter Fried on January 29, 1947. It was a box-office success and was voted the Best Play of the Season by the Drama Critics' Circle.

In recounting the bare facts of his background Miller remarked in passing that in the Presidential campaign of 1932 he favored the Republican candidate. Roosevelt was too "radical," Miller felt; Hoover represented order. And Miller believed in order. The political judgment of the youthful Miller hardly matters, but the impulse it reflects is telling. Miller is a man who desires and requires an ordered, a coherent world.

Miller is a moralist. A moralist is a man who believes he possesses the truth and aims to convince others of it. In Miller this moralistic trait stems from a strong family feeling. In this context the father as prime authority and guide is central. From *The Man Who Had All The Luck* through *Death of A Salesman* the father stands for virtue and value; to his sons he is the personification of Right and Truth. In *All My Sons* Chris cries out against his father's (Joe Keller's) delinquency. "I know you're no worse than other men but I thought you were better. I never saw you as a man; I saw you as my father." Joe Keller expresses Miller's idealization of the father-son relationship when he exclaims, "I'm his father and he's my son. Nothing's bigger than that."

The shock which shatters Miller's dramatic cosmos always begins with the father's inability to enact the role of moral authority the son assigns to him and which the father willy-nilly assumes. The son never altogether absolves the father for his defection nor is the father ever able to forgive himself for it. Each bears a heavy burden of responsibility to the other. Both may be innocent, but both suffer guilt.

The mother, beloved of father and son, supports the paternal legend of "kingship." She is fealty itself. She is unalterably loyal to the family and the ideal of its necessary cohesion as the basis for the good life, a moral world. The mother's devotion to this ideal constitutes a force which is passive in appearance only. Her influence may be constricting, even injurious, though it is never faulted in Miller's plays. Mrs. Keller in *All My Sons* is indirectly the source of much trouble—she preserves the superstitions of the family and of a blemished society—but while Chris rails at his father he barely challenges his mother. Woman in Miller's plays is usually the prop of the male principle without whom man falters, loses his way.

There is something more personal than such general considerations in Miller's view of the family as the "symbolic" cell of the social structure, the dissolution of which is a threat to life itself. It is simply and passionately articulated in *After The Fall* when its central character, Quentin, blurts out, "I can't bear to be a separate person."

Separateness from our fellow men is a human *non sequitur*.

[15]

What in Miller's experience and thought seems the chief cause for the family's crack-up? Where does social fission originate? The Depression of the Thirties was the crucial factor of Miller's formative years; it not only brought hardship to his parents and consequently to their children but it made him realize something else was well. It was not financial stress alone that shook the foundations of American life at that time but a false ideal which the preceding era, the Twenties, had raised to the level of a religious creed: the ideal of Success. The unsuccessful man, the one who failed in business, was a flawed man. Such failure was considered something more than a misfortune; it was the sign of a moral defect. It was turpitude.

Miller has often said that as a college student he was very much affected by a performance of Odets' *Awake and Sing* he saw in Chicago. That play contained a line which struck the keynote of the period: "Go out and fight so life shouldn't be printed on dollar bills," followed by the even more homely precept: "Life should have some dignity."

In *All My Sons* a small town doctor, disappointed in the inspirational meagreness of his practice murmurs, "Money, money, money, money, money. You say it long enough it doesn't mean anything. How I'd love to be around when that happens!" (Mrs. Keller responds with, "You're so childish, Jim.") In *Death Of A Salesman*, Charley, Loman's neighbor, says apropos of Loman, "No man needs only a little salary." And when outraged at Loman's muddle-headedness and feeble sense of reality, his son's basic accusation is that Loman has blown him "full of hot air." It is the hot air of the corrupted American dream, the dream of Success—affluence and status as the ultimate goals of human endeavor.

Willy Loman's worth lies in his natural bent for manual work: he is a craftsman. If he had cultivated that side of himself he might have retained his dignity. But Willy has been seduced by the bitch goddess, Success, by Salesmanship. So he lives in a vacuum, a vapor of meaningless commercial slogans. The irony of Willy's death—his suicide is a distortion of the responsibility he feels toward his son—is embodied in the conviction that only by leaving Biff his insurance money can he fulfill his paternal duty! Willy's hollow "religion" has crippled his faculties, corroded his moral fibre.

Sweet, dumb, nobly ignoble Willy never learns anything. But

[16]

Miller, and the men of his generation, had begun to. Miller became a "radical." The root of evil was the false ideal. The heart of Miller's radicalism is conservative: it seeks the maintenance of individual dignity within the context of the family which broadens to the concept of society as a whole.

The son becomes the father. He desires to take over authority. The radical becomes the leader, the prophet. Armed with a new insight, arrived at through the father's fall, the son now carries the banner of righteousness and justice. He is no longer simply moral; he is a moraliser, a preacher. Thus he may fall from grace into the pit of self-righteousness.

In *All My Sons* Chris says, "Every man follows a star. The star of his honesty. Once it is out it never lights again." It burns so intensely that Chris virtually wills his father's punishment for having knowingly sent out defective airplane motors to the Army.

The severity of such righteousness often boomerangs. The reforms of the Thirties and early Forties were followed by the repressions of the Fifties. Miller spoke out courageously against the forces of repression. *The Crucible* written between 1952 and 1953, is still a virile protest against the aberrations of McCarthyism. That the witchhunt of Salem cannot be equated with the fear of Communism is not valid as a criticism of the play. What *The Crucible* does is to show us a community terrorized into a savagely hysterical fury that is reprehensible whether it is based on fact or on falsehood. The play asks, "Is the accuser always holy now?", a question altogether suitable to the situation of the Fifties. "Vengeance is walking Salem" had become almost literally exact.

The hindsight afforded by *After The Fall* renders perceptible certain secondary aspects of *The Crucible* which passed unnoticed at the time of its production in 1953. Neither John Proctor nor his wife Elizabeth is guilty of witchcraft! Both act in the upright manner we expect of them. (Miller, found guilty of Contempt of Congress in 1956 for refusing to mention the names of people he recognized at a Communist meeting he had attended some years before, was cleared of the charge by the United States Court of Appeals in 1958.) But other guilts are confessed by the Proctors, man and wife, in *The Crucible*. Elizabeth has been guilty of coldness to her husband; John

[17]

of "lechery." He has been unfaithful. Both suspect that part of their misfortune, the accusation of conspiring with the Devil, and their inability to clear themselves are somehow due to their private failings.

One of the most unmistakable features of Miller's work, as we have noted, is what might be called its moralism, or if you will, its Puritanism. There is a traditional sort of tenderness, even a trace of sentimentality, in the early Miller plays. The woman is sweetly yearned for and serves as mate and mainstay to keep her man confident. There is little or no hint of any sensual appreciation of woman. In *Death Of A Salesman* Biff feels nothing but horror at Willy's pathetic fling on the road. Desire plays little part in the configuration of dramatic elements in any of Miller's plays before *The Crucible* and enters the scene obliquely and, as it were, shamefacedly as a prop to the plot in *A View From The Bridge*.

The Puritan conscience is a complex phenomenon. Even while it holds fast to its conviction of rightness, it is haunted by a need for the expiation of its own sins. There is nothing for which it feels itself entirely blameless. Man must pay and pay and pay—for everything. The ever-fortunate youth in *The Man Who Had All The Luck* does not consider himself safe until he suffers a most damaging defeat. His partial but painful setback is a warrant to him that he may go forward in his life with some degree of assurance that no greater disaster will befall him. What the Puritan hankers for is total innocence, and it torments him to understand that it cannot possibly be achieved.

Even the pursuit of righteousness and truth seems to the thoroughgoing Puritan a virtuous aggressiveness which is itself not wholly innocent. It may mask a drive for power. Thus Biff in *Salesman*, as later Quentin in *After The Fall*, questions his own good faith. Sue Bayliss, the down-to-earth doctor's wife in *All My Sons*, wants Chris, avenging angel or conscience of the play, to move away from the neighborhood. "Chris," she says, "makes people want to be better than it is possible to be . . . I resent being next door to the Holy Family. It makes me feel like a bum." The sentiment is psychologically and sociologically sound—reformers disturb public quiet—but what is especially to be remarked here is that in all his plays Miller gives evidence of wanting to move away from himself in this regard. It worries him that he sits in judgment, that he is placing himself in a position to which he has no right. It is as if Miller felt himself a Reverend Davidson who anticipates and desires his own humbling.

To speak of this aspect of Miller's artistic physiognomy as a flaw would be to miss the tension which gives Miller's work its peculiar fascination. The wish to expiate sins of pride, bad faith or moral arrogance are related to a sense of responsibility which lends stature to Miller's work and makes it intimately moving. We are not, we must not be, separate one from the other. Our refusal to acknowledge this and to act upon it is the sin which secretly torments us and causes us profound grief.

Miller harbors an abiding affection for his least striking play, *A Memory of Two Mondays*. This is understandable because in this play he seems at rest, relaxed from the strictures of his central theme. In this play he recalls without blame or debate the simple, undemanding, unselfconsciously oppressed folk with whom he worked at the Tenth Avenue warehouse before he entered the world of assertion and moral combat. Here he dwelled without the exposing glare of critical self-examination. The warehouse, gehenna of purposeless toil, was his paradise; like infancy, it was free from the burden of ethical choice.

The repose of this short play is followed immediately by the travail of *A View From The Bridge*, the last of Miller's plays before the "silent" years. In a sense this play is an adjunct to *The Crucible*. While the blemish on Proctor's purity is a contributing factor to his calvary, the personal motivation in *A View From The Bridge* obscures its theme almost as much as it reveals it. For this play dramatizes the passion of betrayal. A decent man is led to squealing on his kin because of jealousy.

Eddie Carbone does not recognize his motivation; this would mortify him. He must rationalize his act on moral grounds. So much is made of Carbone's adulterous and semi-incestuous drive towards his niece that we are apt to miss the fact that what is at stake is not the psychology of sexual turmoil but of duplicity, the man's inability to live up to the obligations of comradeship. We must not force others to pay for the agony of our own weakness.

Miller is compassionate with Carbone; yet he is angry with him. He is compassionate because he feels in himself the bewilderment involved in the sexual impulse, particularly when repressed; he is angry because Carbone is a liar as all men are who conceal their confusion or corruption in an honorable cloak. Miller not only implies that Carbone craves punishment for his delation, he also believes Carbone deserves death. Still Miller, as a humane Puritan, shrinks from so full a measure of condemnation—"an eye for an eye"—and he has his "chorus," in the person of Alfieri, the lawyer-narrator, say, "Most of the time now we settle for half. And I like it better." One suspects that Alfieri says this with a certain trembling as if he were not certain that he does "like it better," that Alfieri feels that the terrible justice which slays Carbone or has him slay himself is the nobler.

We must resume a listing of further biographical data. Miller was married to Mary Slattery, a fellow student at the University of Michigan, in 1942. She bore him two children: a girl now nineteen and a boy sixteen. He divorced Mary Miller in 1956. He then married Marilyn Monroe. He wrote *The Misfits* for her, a film about the lone worker in a society of industrial mass production. It is a film, he admits, marred by too many cross-purposes. (*The Misfits* was the only one of Miller's film scripts to go before the cameras. Another, called *The Hook*, written with Elia Kazan's encouragement, dealt with racketeering on the waterfront and was about to be produced by Columbia Pictures. The production was abandoned when pressure from certain unions in the film industry was brought to bear on the picture company.) After his divorce from Marilyn Monroe, Miller married Inge Morath, an Austrian-born photographer, in 1961. A daughter, Rebecca, was born to them in 1962.

Two features of *After The Fall* are immediately noticeable. It is the first of Miller's plays where the main emphasis is almost entirely personal. It is also the first Miller play where the largest part of the action concerns itself with marital relationships.

Still *After The Fall* is not only an extension of the themes to be found in Miller's previous plays; it is a reaffirmation through a reversal. The strenuous moralist, the man whose family—the mother in particular—dedicated him to great accomplishments, has come to the middle point of his life and brings himself to trial. He not only confesses, he accuses himself. The jury is his *alter ego*—in the audience; the evidence is provided by the testimony of his memory. His self-assurance has gone. As many in our time, he is "hung up"; he despairs.

He now finds the continuous "litigation of existence" pointless because the judge's seat is empty. There is no "father," no supreme arbiter. He will have to allow us, the audience, to judge him. Why is the trial held? Not so that he may be condemned or that the charges brought be dismissed but so that he regain his capacity to "move on." He is seeking the hope which lies beyond despair, the life which renews itself after the fall, with the death of the old self. He wants to bury himself as an Idea and find himself as a Person.

The lawyer, Quentin, who was sent forth in his youth with a Mission to fulfill a destiny in the light of some "star," now begins to recollect the specific circumstances of his past—people and events—instead of patterning them on a principle. "To see endangers principle," he says. The examination of conscience through a review of the precise detail in the crisis of his life exposes his self-delusions, hypocrisies, insufficiencies, falterings and confusions. He is now skeptical of abstracts, even the abstract of Despair.

The tangle of lives in the play's broad canvas, the complexity and contradiction of motives in his former search for a moral victory lead him to an understanding of his, and possibly our universal, complicity in wrongdoing. We who denounce the hangman are ourselves executioners. We assume powers we do not possess. We undertake tasks it is not within our means to complete. The proposition that we are not separate takes on a new meaning; a new light is shed on the injunction of human responsibility. Each of us is separate and in our separateness we must assume responsibility even in full awareness of that separateness.

Thus Quentin may survive after the fall through a recognition of his own place among the accused, a realization of his role as an accomplice in the misdeeds he has denounced. The judge's bench is not on high; it is in the common court of our lives together. We are all both the jailers and prisoners of the concentration camps. The acceptance of the defeat in this realization may liberate the man dogged by having had "all the luck"—and answers! There are no guarantees for any choice we make, but one is never absolved from the necessity of making choices and of paying for them.

The struggle represented in all of Miller's work, of which *After The Fall* is a central turning point, achieves a special eloquence for us in the American particularity of its tone and speech. There is a plainness, a kind of neighborhood friendliness and good humor, one might say a saving ordinariness, which gives Miller's dialogue a special appeal. The literary or aesthetic "purist" who deplores this element of Miller's talent is as remote from our reality as those who once found nothing more in Huckleberry Finn than a story for kids.

Miller is a popular writer. This may be a limitation but it is more probably a strength. Those who wept over Willy Loman, whether his story exemplifies true Tragedy or not, are closer to the truth of our day than those who want it told to them in monumental or quasi-mythical symbols for all time.

There is besides the comforting familiarity of Miller's expression an enthusiasm which mingles a deep-rooted American idealism with an age-old Hebraic fervor, a quality which mounts from hearth and home to the elevation of an altar. Miller's dialogue, coined from the energetic and flavorsome palaver of the streets, is finally wrought into something close to prophetic incantation.

After The Fall is a signal step in the evolution of Arthur Miller as man and artist. The play's auto-criticism exposes him to us; it also liberates him so that he can go on free of false legend and heavy halo. Had he not written this play he might never have been able to write another. We may now look to a future of ever more creative effort.

*On the back of a snapshot: "Gene and Carlotta—Cap d'Ail,
France, January 1929"—one year after the premiere of*
Marco Millions.

Eugene O'Neill and "Marco Millions"
by Arthur and Barbara Gelb

IT IS FORTY-FOUR YEARS since Eugene O'Neill took his place in the professional theatre, shaking Broadway out of its doldrums of bedroom farces and simple-minded melodramas. With the presentation of his first full-length play, *Beyond the Horizon*, at the old Morosco in 1920, a new era in native American drama began, an era in which our theatre grew into an art form that, perhaps, will have its fulfillment in such endeavors as the Lincoln Center's repertory company.

O'Neill, whose own vision of repertory was frustrated during his lifetime, in effect created the climate and paved the way for a group like the Lincoln Center theatre. It was O'Neill's dream, soon after he had established himself as a force in the theatre, to create a repertory company that would embrace and perpetuate his works along with those of other serious-minded dramatists. Without conceit, but with a confident evaluation of his contribution to the literature of the stage, he envisioned a repertory company that would periodically revive the bulk of his enormous output, not merely the plays that had been popular successes. He outlined a detailed plan for such a theatre, but financial support never materialized.

O'Neill would have been pleased that Lincoln Center was able to risk putting on *Marco Millions* as the first of his plays. He always believed *Marco* had been neglected unjustly and he longed for it to have an active place among his representative works.

It is true that *Marco Millions* has been overshadowed by other O'Neill plays. This is justifiable in the case of his four greatest tragedies: *Desire Under The Elms, Mourning Becomes Electra, The Ice-*

man Cometh and *Long Day's Journey Into Night*. But *Marco* certainly ranks with such better known works as *The Hairy Ape*, *The Emperor Jones* and *SS Glencairn*. *Marco*'s tragic love story is every bit as poignant as that of *Beyond The Horizon*; its theme is more meaningful in contemporary terms than that of *The Great God Brown*; and it is far more daring in form and expression than the once hugely popular *Anna Christie*. It also marks a significant phase in O'Neill's life and art.

One reason why it was relegated to obscurity from the beginning is that its original production, January 9, 1928, was followed within three weeks by *Strange Interlude*, which startled audiences with its sensational psycho-sexual theme. Another reason is that *Marco Millions* was not produced with anything like the poetic grandeur that O'Neill had conceived for it. Having been, like most enduring works of art, much ahead of its time in both artistic concept and stage technique, it was tepidly received thirty-seven years ago in a theatre that was uncomfortable in the presence of poetic tragedy.

O'Neill was just under thirty-five when he began writing *Marco Millions*. As with many of his other plays, he had had the idea some years earlier. *Strange Interlude* was brewing in his mind at the same time, but the only similarity between the two plays was a structural one. O'Neill had by then conceived the idea of writing a double- or triple-length play that would pound audiences out of their traditional passivity. Although *Marco* was originally written as two full-length plays to be performed consecutively, O'Neill eventually decided to condense it. *Strange Interlude* was the work that emerged as the author's initial experiment in marathon plays.

When O'Neill drafted *Marco* in the summer of 1923, he was living in an isolated cabin at the edge of the ocean in Provincetown, Mass., where he and his second wife, Agnes, had been spending several months a year since 1919. The cabin, abandoned by the Coast Guard because of its proximity to the encroaching Atlantic, had been a wedding gift to O'Neill from his father. James O'Neill was a flamboyant touring actor, who achieved great popular success during the last quarter of the 19th Century, but who never fulfilled the artistic promise he had shown as a young man. James had been dead for three years when his son set to work on *Marco Millions*; he had lived long enough to see the premiere of *Beyond the Horizon*. O'Neill was still haunted by his father's ghost, and still preoccupied in his writing with his ambivalent relationship to James, as he had been in *Beyond the Horizon* and would continue to be in most of his major works to come.

O'Neill believed he could draw an incisive parallel between the 13th Century Venetian merchant, Marco Polo, and the typical 20th Century American businessman, who preferred the pursuit of materialism to the cultivation of the soul. Like all the other abstractions that held O'Neill's interest, this one had grown directly out of painful observation of his father. Technically not a businessman, his father did manage his own touring company, invested in numerous commercial ventures and was more interested in accumulating cash than in serving art.

James O'Neill presented to his colleagues a convivial, generous and serene exterior. But he was, in fact, a bedeviled man. Having spent an impoverished childhood as the son of an immigrant Irish family in the Midwest, James became obsessed with the pursuit of financial security. The obsession shadowed his son's life and was an oft-repeated theme of O'Neill's plays.

James was forty-two when Eugene was born on October 16, 1888. He had been living for several years with the uneasy knowledge that his chance at artistic greatness had passed. A gifted Shakespearean actor, he had once dreamed of inheriting Edwin Booth's position in the American theatre. But when he was 37 and on the verge of becoming established as a classical actor, he was offered the leading role in a new stage adaptation of *The Count of Monte Cristo*. His popular success in the role was instantaneous and the lure of the money to be made proved irresistible. James tried from time to time to return to Shakespeare, but audiences would no longer accept him in classical roles. He was trapped. *The Count of Monte Cristo* proved to be one of the most durable vehicles in the history of the American theatre. Year after year James toured the United States as Edmond Dantes, continuing to draw huge audiences and earn vast sums of money even after the role had become a melancholy mockery in his own eyes.

Eugene O'Neill's mother, Ella, an emotionally fragile woman with a mystical turn of mind, had long since been worn down by the hectic life of a touring actor's wife. Her ten-year-old son, James, Jr., was in boarding school when Eugene was born in a Manhattan hotel room. A second son, Edmund, had died in infancy. Ella felt guilty about them both, blaming her lack of a settled home, and James' inability and unwillingness to provide one, for the death of one child and the enforced banishment of the other. She did not welcome Eugene's birth; he was another infant to drag from town to town until old enough to be placed in boarding school—another guilt for which to blame herself and reproach her husband.

Eugene seemed to absorb this atmosphere of guilt and frustration from the moment he was born. His childhood instilled in him a sense of loneliness and impermanence engendered by stuffy trains, shabby hotel rooms and countless chilly dressing rooms. As an adolescent on vacation from school, he discovered that his mother was a narcotics addict and that she blamed the habit on the burden of his birth. In his turn, O'Neill assumed his share of the family guilt. His constant conflict over whether to blame his father or his mother, his love for and fury toward them both, reflected itself in a brooding, withdrawn personality, explosive rages and an urge toward self-destructive action.

Before he was twenty-one he had become an episodic drunkard, had flunked out of college, made a hasty and foolish marriage, fathered a child whom he was neither emotionally nor financially equipped to support and had been sent on a rather pointless mining expedition in the Honduran jungles by James in the hope of straightening him out.

At twenty-one, Eugene had a radically different idea from his father about what to do with his life. James, reluctantly admitting that he had let greatness slip by, nevertheless took a dogged pride in the fact that he had worked conscientiously and hard in his profession, that he was a responsible citizen, a provident father and a devoted, if demanding, husband. Eugene's shiftlessness angered and depressed him. A hearty drinker himself, but one who could hold his liquor, he deplored Eugene's protracted descents into alcoholism and near-dereliction.

James scoffed at his son's exultation in his sea adventures, which followed soon after his return from Honduras: a stint as an ordinary seaman on a Norwegian barque, a promotion to Able-bodied Seaman on a tramp ship and a brief but lusty voyage to London and back on an ocean liner. James was still inclined to regard him as a dabbler when Eugene, at twenty-eight, having won a bout with tuberculosis and served a brief term as a reporter, began to receive recognition for the early sea plays based on his experiences, for the material rewards from the plays, as produced in the tiny Provincetown Playhouse in Greenwich Village, were meager.

The climax of the conflict between the father's materialism and the son's determination to pursue art for art's sake came on James' deathbed when he conceded that Eugene showed talent and that he himself had wasted his.

"I can die happy because I think Gene is going to be all right," James said to a relative after being told of his son's Pulitzer Prize for *Beyond the Horizon* in the summer of 1920. And to his son, with his last breath, he murmured, "Eugene—I'm going to a better sort of life—this sort of life—here—all froth—no good—rottenness!"

Eugene indicated how strongly his father's dying words had affected him in a letter to a friend:

> *My father died broken, unhappy, intensely bitter, feeling that life was "a damned hard billet to chew." This after seventy-six years of what the mob undoubtedly regard as a highly successful career! It furnishes food for thought, what? . . . his (dying) words . . . are written indelibly—seared on my brain—a warning from the Beyond to remain true to the best that is in me though the heavens fall.*

O'Neill lived his own life by these words; and it is this theme that he pursued in *Marco Millions*.

While James O'Neill's personality and career provided the point of departure for his son's conception of Marco Polo, there were, as with all of O'Neill's plays, many other elements involved, some of them purely imaginative and unconscious and others loosely based on history and deliberately diabolical. For example, O'Neill took delight in the similarity of names between Kubla Khan and the celebrated financier, Otto Kahn, to whom he sarcastically referred as the Great Kahn. Though his interest in the arts was generous, Otto Kahn did not measure up to O'Neill's ideal for millionaires, which was to put the bulk of their wealth at the disposal of artists with no strings attached. Otto Kahn had once solemnly asked O'Neill to write a play about businessmen and *Marco* was, in part, O'Neill's tongue-in-cheek compliance with that request.

Marco is the story of a young man intent on amassing a fortune, and blind and deaf to the beauty, tenderness and spiritual wisdom he encounters on his voyages. He cannot perceive the sacrificial love held for him by a beautiful princess, the granddaughter of the mighty Kubla Khan; he cannot recognize the mockery with which the Khan regards his swashbuckling airs as he grows ever more prosperous and fat-souled; and he is fretful and half-asleep in the presence of sages, philosophers and priests.

A kind of Babbitt, he continues to thrive, unaware of the pity, contempt or despair he inspires in the course of his stolid march toward material success. In the end, he returns to Venice a millionaire to marry the blowsy, middle-aged sweetheart of his youth, smugly certain that he has attained the best of all possible worlds.

O'Neill's satire is broad and at times a trifle heavy-handed, but there is also fine poetry in the work, and compassion, not to mention an amusing and inventive epilogue, which was not included in the original production. O'Neill's script called for the house lights to come up at once after the final scene and, presumably, for the actors to defer their curtain calls as a man, seated in the aisle of the first row, stretched, yawned and rose to leave.

"Although there is nothing out of the ordinary in his actions, his appearance excites general comment and surprise," O'Neill wrote hopefully, "for he is dressed as a Venetian merchant of the later Thirteenth Century. In fact, it is none other than Marco Polo himself, looking a bit sleepy, a trifle puzzled and not a little irritated as his thoughts, in spite of himself, cling for a passing moment to the play just ended. He appears quite unaware of being unusual and walks in the crowd without self-consciousness, very much as one of them. Arrived in the lobby his face begins to clear of all disturbing memories of what had happened on the stage. The noise, the lights of the streets, recall him at once to himself. Impatiently he waits for his car, casting a glance here and there at faces in the groups around him, his eyes impersonally speculative, his bearing stolid with the dignity of one who is sure of his place in the world. His car, a luxurious limousine, draws up at the curb. He gets in briskly, the door is slammed, the car edges away into the traffic and Marco Polo, with a satisfied sigh at the sheer comfort of it all, resumes his life."

O'Neill was a tenacious dramatist; he was always seeking ways of pressing his plays more intimately and vividly into the hearts and minds of his audiences, forcing them to carry something vital and moving away from the theatre with them. He wanted his audiences to participate, literally, in the dramatic experience. O'Neill wrote this epilogue in a day when thrust stages, open arenas and actors' entrances and exits through the aisles of the auditorium were not part of the American theatrical convention. The epilogue was a defiant, symbolical demonstration of how it could be done if only a producer had the imagination to do it.

Despite what O'Neill regarded as the shortcomings of the original production, such as the cutting of certain characters and scenes, *Marco Millions* received a number of moderately enthusiastic reviews. They did not please O'Neill, who had little respect for the intelligence of most critics. When they praised a play of his, he usually muttered that it was for the wrong reasons; when they condemned, he blamed it on their personal vindictiveness, or ulcers. His stock reaction to critics in general was, "I'd like to break every bone in their heads."

The premiere of *Marco Millions* took place on January 9, 1928. It had been released for publication almost a year earlier by O'Neill, who had grown tired of waiting for a producer to mount it. Such praise as there was went largely to the cast headed by Alfred Lunt as Marco, and including Margalo Gilmore, Morris Carnovsky, Mary Blair and Dudley Digges. O'Neill wasted little energy in sulking over the play's fate. It had opened during a time of personal crisis, and he stayed in New York only long enough to see *Strange Interlude* launched on January 30, then departed for Europe for what was to be a period of self-imposed exile, lasting more than three years.

O'Neill had fallen in love with Carlotta Monterey, a former actress and a celebrated beauty. He left his wife and two young children in Bermuda, and headed, guiltily but joyously, for what he envisioned as an idyllic new life abroad. For a time, in spite of a divorce scandal, problems about his children and the much publicized suicide of Carlotta's former husband, Ralph Barton, O'Neill seemed to have found the idyll of love and work he sought.

After marrying Carlotta, he wrote the masterful *Mourning Becomes Electra* and the tender comedy, *Ah, Wilderness!*, and, having built himself a secluded house in Georgia, settled down to write the eleven-play cycle dealing with an American family that was to be his masterwork. The cycle occupied him intensively for the next several years. He was still working on it when, in 1936, he became the first American dramatist to win the Nobel Prize. But by that time, his health was already beginning to fail and he could not even make the ceremonial journey to Sweden to accept the award.

In search of a drier climate and medical treatment, O'Neill and Carlotta moved to California, where, once again, they built themselves an isolated home. O'Neill's health worsened and he found the physical effort of writing increasingly difficult. World War II threw him into a state of deep mental gloom and, with its gasoline rationing and dearth of servants, made it impossible for Carlotta to run her house and get proper medical treatment for her husband.

O'Neill unhappily shelved the massive outlines, notes and half-completed manuscripts of his cycle, having finished only one play to his satisfaction, *A Touch of the Poet*. Sensing that he would not have time to complete the other cycle plays, he turned, instead, to the writing of three plays he felt more urgently needed expression: his two masterpieces, *The Iceman Cometh* and *Long Day's Journey Into Night* and the somewhat less statuesque, but imposing sequel to *Long Day's Journey*, *A Moon for the Misbegotten*.

O'Neill wrote nothing from 1943 until his death, ten years later. The undiagnosed disease from which he suffered, while leaving his brain cruelly alert, affected his nervous system to such a degree that he could not grasp a pencil in his hand or walk without stumbling. His final years were bitter. Though he had three plays completed, only one, *The Iceman Cometh*, was produced in New York before his death, and it was not appreciated in the cynical, arid, post-war year of 1946. *A Moon for the Misbegotten* was a miscast failure on the road. And O'Neill refused to allow the revealingly autobiographical *Long Day's Journey* to be produced before his death.

A number of prominent critics began attacking O'Neill as over-rated and relegated him to quick obscurity. Few theatres in the United States were reviving his plays, and in New York City, where Shaw and Ibsen and Chekhov were frequently being done, an O'Neill revival was a rarity.

[32]

With his income depleted, he took refuge in a modest house overlooking the Atlantic, not too far from Boston where medical help was readily available. There, he brooded, refusing to see most of his old friends, suffering physically and mentally and quarrelling with his wife, herself under an almost unendurable strain.

O'Neill's despair reached its climax when his elder son, of whom he had been fond and proud, committed suicide at forty. The tension between O'Neill and Carlotta erupted in the winter of 1951 and they separated for several months. By the time they were reunited, O'Neill was an obviously dying man.

In the hotel suite he and Carlotta took in Boston, O'Neill tore his unfinished cycle plays into bits. At his request, she burned them.

O'Neill's death on November 27, 1953, caused little of the stir that usually attends the passing of a literary giant. It is true that New York City was having a newspaper strike, but obituaries in the journals of other cities were meager. Europe on the other hand, notably Sweden, felt the significance of his death. O'Neill had always been held in higher esteem abroad than in his own country.

It was not until 1956, when *The Iceman Cometh* was brilliantly resurrected off Broadway and *Long Day's Journey Into Night* was published, that interest in O'Neill gained momentum. Since then, not a season has gone by without an O'Neill revival either on or off Broadway. In the decade since his death, O'Neill's countrymen have learned to value him more than they did in his lifetime.

S. N. Behrman "... *his eyes twinkling with conspiratorial friendliness as if to enlist you in a cabal against whatever is pompous and dull-witted in life.*"

S. N. Behrman: A Dialogue
with John Simon

S. N. Behrman's name in the American theatre has always been associated with charm and grace buttressed with shrewdness and common sense, qualities no less apparent in his biographical and autobiographical writings and in his conversation. It seemed, therefore, appropriate to let Sam Behrman extend his frolicsome canniness to the areas of criticism and self-criticism as well, by simply letting him talk about his work, the work of others and the world he has been living in. It turned out to be something nicer than an interview: a visit. Charm was all around: in the extremely pretty secretary; in Behrman's embroidered, red, oriental slippers; in the man himself, a cheerfully fleshy owl—unassuming, amiable, full of tart merriment and irresistible candor. I cannot reproduce here his laugh, probably the most guileless and hearty I have ever heard, or his eyes twinkling with conspiratorial friendliness as if to enlist you in a cabal against whatever is pompous and dull-witted in life. But, at least, I can tell you what was said.

SIMON: Mr. Behrman, how would you describe your work? What kind of plays would you say you write?

BEHRMAN: Well, I write plays about people who are fairly intelligent. I'm not a proletarian writer. Did you ever hear the story which I love that Molnár told me? In the great days in Budapest there was a woman who always sat in the royal box at first nights. She was very highly placed and she'd come in dressed in diadems and all kinds of jewels. One night there was a play like *The Lower Depths*—a proletarian play—and everybody was miserable, terribly unhappy, the walls were peeling, hopeless from the

[35]

start. When the curtain came down, somebody asked her how she liked it, and she said indignantly, "It's not a play for a first night."

SIMON: Do you write plays for first nights?

BEHRMAN: No, I don't write plays for first nights. My first play . . . I was very young and living in an unheated room on 23rd Street, penniless and quite desperate, and I had printed a short story in *The Smart Set* magazine which was then edited by Mencken and Nathan, and I got a very nice letter from George Jean Nathan and a check for $50. He said he'd like to see more, and that it seemed dramatic to him. I was in this room and I had no idea for anything new. In three weeks I dramatized the story, and that was my first play, *The Second Man*. It was successful here and in London. The way I got the idea for the short story was by coming across in my reading a sentence by Lord Leighton in which he spoke of the duality of his own nature. At that time I didn't know who on earth Lord Leighton was, but this sentence struck me and I wrote a play based on it. So, you see, I'm interested in what problems afflict mature and intelligent people. I think they have problems, too. I think they suffer, too. Have I defined my work?

SIMON: Well, it's the beginning of a definition, anyway. Did you then, to start with, not think of becoming a playwright?

BEHRMAN: No, I wanted to write prose. That was my passion in my youth and I just couldn't make a living out of it. I had quite a few things published in *The Smart Set* within, I'd say, a period of five or six years—maybe ten things—and in those days that was like getting something in *The New Yorker*. But I think $50 was the most I got, and then came the accident of my dramatizing that short story.

SIMON: Don't I recall your having done some kind of playwriting before *The Second Man*?

BEHRMAN: I took Professor Baker's course at Harvard and I wrote one play that got me a job in New York as press agent for a play that lasted two weeks, and I wrote various plays that never got anywhere. But what I really wanted to do was to write prose. I still do and I hope to devote the rest of my life, whatever there's

[36]

left of it, to writing prose. I don't think I'll try a play again after this one.

SIMON: When you say "prose," I take it you don't mean such things as your biographical writings on Beerbohm and Duveen, but fiction.

BEHRMAN: Yes. I have been working for several years in what time I have on a novel. It's a novel the idea for which I have carried around for 25 years. I've done some work on it and I hope to finish it before I die.

SIMON: I'm sure you will. Though they are always deflecting your attention from it. Luring you to Hollywood, and—

BEHRMAN: Well, I don't get many Hollywood offers any more. At the moment I am working on a film treatment, but it's the first picture offer I've had in years, and Hollywood isn't what it was.

SIMON: You aren't fond of Hollywood, are you?

BEHRMAN: Oh, I'm very happy not to be in it.

SIMON: But what about that musical, *The Legendary Mizners*?

BEHRMAN: *The Legendary Mizners* I worked out with George Kaufman and Irving Berlin. It looked like a lightning thing, but the antagonism between Berlin and Kaufman was so acute—and so very funny. I've spent a great deal of time on ventures like that which never come to anything. Just never come to anything.

SIMON: We all think of you as a writer of comedies, but you did in fact write a couple of non-comic plays, which, I believe, didn't go over very well.

BEHRMAN: What were they?

SIMON: *Dunningan's Daughter*, for instance.

BEHRMAN: Well, yes, that was the most disastrous failure I ever had in my life, and there's a story behind that. That play started as a comedy, but was deflected by the forces that take place in the theatre, and the protagonist of that force deflected that play . . . I mean a very famous man who now admits—is good enough to admit—that he ruined that play for me. And then *The Talley Method*, I suppose, was in a way a serious play, and that, too, failed. But it had a good first act and Ina Claire was wonderful. But, mostly, I want to write comedy: comedy of my own kind. Now, *Biography* was a successful comedy, but it's really a tragic play, don't you think?

[37]

SIMON: I would say it is a serious comedy.

BEHRMAN: Actually, I believe that every comedy has a tragic background—a serious part. Now, *End of Summer*—have you read *End of Summer*?

SIMON: Yes. I think that's my favorite.

BEHRMAN: It's my favorite, too. I think it's the best play I ever wrote. Well, that also is a comedy. It certainly got terrific laughs, but it's a serious play. How would you classify my new one, *But For Whom Charlie*?

SIMON: I would say that that is a serious play with comic overtones, rather than a comic play with serious overtones.

BEHRMAN: Yes, I think you're right. I think in a way it's the most serious play I've ever written.

SIMON: Now then, how do these comedies come out of you, Mr. Behrman? Do you decide, "I want to write this kind of play," or does the play write itself?

BEHRMAN: The play writes itself. Take *End of Summer*. I knew an enchanting woman who was very sweet to me when I was nobody. One of the dearest women I've ever known and an incorrigible romantic. She fell in love with the wrong men, one after the other. She eventually committed suicide; there was no way of stopping her. She was married to a rich man who had a country house, and I was just nobody around town, trying to get somewhere, and her kindness to me was extraordinary. She had me up to this country house all the time. Many famous people came there, which is where I first met the celebrities of that era. Alexander Woollcott, Frank Adams and all of them. Well, when she died, I said, "Why did this darling have to die?" and I realized that she just was incapable of criticizing any impulse she had in the direction of love. All she lived for was love and she was totally unlucky in the men she chose. They all used her and discarded her. *End of Summer* came from that character, that woman.

SIMON: And did she also have a daughter, like Paula in the play, or was that your invention?

BEHRMAN: That was an invention. She had no children.

SIMON: May I assume, then, that there's a fairly strong biographical, or autobiographical, note in your work?

BEHRMAN: I think there is in all my plays. There couldn't fail to be. Although some people think the plays are paradoxical considering my early environment, my childhood, was poverty-stricken.

SIMON: Yes, I was going to ask you about that.

BEHRMAN: It's just that when I was very young I loved Max Beerbohm. It's just the only thing that interests me: conversation.

SIMON: Until you wrote *The Worcester Account*, did it ever occur to you to write about your background?

BEHRMAN: Never. And it was an accident that I wrote *The Worcester Account*.

SIMON: Was it a voluntary act with you, then, "I will write about sparkling and witty and charming people?"

BEHRMAN: No. As I told you, *The Second Man* was suggested to me by that wonderful sentence of Lord Leighton. I was very young and it appealed to me. It struck me, because I must have been conscious of the duality in my own nature, and there was no way of writing that except as high comedy. So that struck my note, so to speak. The next play I did was a dramatization of an English novel which was signed, "By a lady of quality"—the novel, that is.

SIMON: That was *Serena Blandish* by Enid Bagnold?

BEHRMAN: I never knew about whom it was, never knew anything about it, but the theme of it, the idea of a really darling girl in a corrupt society who hasn't got the equipment to cope with that corrupt society because her nature is essentially candid and outgiving, appealed to me. And you couldn't write that unless you made it extremely articulate. The next play I wrote I was too young to write; it was called *Meteor*, a study in egomania, which has always interested me. I'm not an egomaniac myself, but I had to deal with one when I was press agent for Jed Harris. He was an egomaniac. So I wrote a satire on egomania. And you couldn't write that, except—forgive me, if it sounds priggish—except in cultivated dialogue. It required the kind of dialogue that I like to read myself.

SIMON: Does this bring us to the influences on your work?

BEHRMAN: Yes. When I met GBS in 1944, I said to him, "You ruined my life." He asked, "How?" I said, "When I was a kid in Worcester, Massachusetts, I went by streetcar, which it was possible to do then, to Boston. I saw Forbes-Robertson and Gertrude Elliott in *Caesar and Cleopatra*, and I thought how marvelous it was." I don't think it's so marvelous now, but I did then, and I thought the whole theatre was like that. And then I went back to Worcester and got all Shaw out of the library and kept reading it. Reading Shaw, being immersed in Shaw as I was, influenced me a great deal.

SIMON: How would you say the basic idea for a play presents itself to you? Is it through a person you meet or think of, or through a concept that occurs to you?

BEHRMAN: I'll tell you. Sometimes it's just a phrase. I wrote a play called *Brief Moment*, not at all a very good play, but a sentence I had written had the words, "brief moment," in it and I wrote a play around that sentence. I don't think that would happen again, but an idea will start a play for me.

SIMON: Let's take another example. How about *Rain From Heaven*?

BEHRMAN: Well, I'm a Jew and I was tremendously affected by what was happening in the world. Also, I was in England, and Elizabeth Bibesco, to whom the play is dedicated—she's Asquith's daughter—told me a great deal about Ernst Toller; she was wonderful about him. The woman in that play is really Elizabeth Bibesco, a liberal Englishwoman of the best kind. So that was how that play got going.

SIMON: What about that man in *But For Whom Charlie*, the writer who can no longer write? That seems based on someone.

BEHRMAN: The writer who no longer writes? I briefly knew Scott Fitzgerald in Hollywood and—do you remember the incident in *But For Whom Charlie* when the old man tells about reading his obituary? Yes? Let me tell you what happened. I was very persona grata in Hollywood, I'm ashamed to tell you, with the triumvirate at Metro-Goldwyn-Mayer in its great days, and one of that triumvirate was a fellow named Bernie Hyman. I had a lunch date with him one day and I came into his office and saw this sheet of yellow paper headed. "Writers Available" and I ran through this list. I saw the name Scott Fitzgerald and my heart sank because it was a necrologue, that list. Because the one thing in Hollywood you must not be is "available." If you're "available" they do not want you; they want to know, "Why is he available?" I won't tell you now of the efforts I made to get Scott jobs. They said he's too slow, he's this, that and the other. Well, that made an indelible impression on me. Scott was not writing and there's nothing so awful, as you know. And maybe there's a fear of when I will be unable to write—because there'd be very little left in my life. So perhaps that scene is autobiographical, too.

SIMON: Well, since you did somehow wander into playwriting, are you glad that you did, or do you think that what with lists like that in the show-business world, it would have been better to stick to fiction?

BEHRMAN: I feel that if I'd been able to manage it, to stick to fiction, I might have done fairly well and I would have been spared the terrors that afflict the theatre—especially for the last ten years. Because I think there is no theatre in this country.

SIMON: We'll get to that in a minute. But first, what is it that you find you can do in fiction that you couldn't do in the theatre?

BEHRMAN: For one thing, I can work by myself, and when the book is done, if it's any good, that's it. I don't have to put it into the Broadway market. I don't have to worry: no actor has to read it, no manager has to read it, just the publisher. I think I'm quite critical, and if I feel that I have succeeded in doing it, then I'm justified in publishing it. I won't have to worry about anybody else because the theatre is a collaboration from beginning to end and it depends on a tremendous number of imponderables.

SIMON: Do you feel that some of your plays, besides *Dunnigan's Daughter*, have been changed more than you would have liked?

BEHRMAN: Yes, they have been. I've had plays on the road, for instance *The Cold Wind and the Warm*. I think if that had closed on the road and I'd worked on it for six months, I might have gotten a good play out of it, but you can't do that: you've got an opening date booked in New York. One of the things I like about Lincoln Center is that writers will not be under that kind of pressure.

SIMON: How does this pressure work, Mr. Behrman? After all, the

Dramatists' Guild contract stipulates that you, the playwright, must have the last word.

BEHRMAN: Oh, that is so, but it never works out that way.

SIMON: How do you get robbed of your last word?

BEHRMAN: It happens because you're in Philadelphia, say, which I was, and you get bad notices and panic sets in. You see, these things are all done, mostly, under panic conditions.

SIMON: Is there no such thing as the playwright asserting himself and saying, "These Philadelphia reviewers don't know what they're talking about?"

BEHRMAN: Well, there are very few heroes among playwrights.

SIMON: As among other men.

BEHRMAN: As among other men. And the playwright has a sneaking suspicion that the critics are right. And the conditions of a road tour in the contemporary theatre are such that you simply cannot function at your best.

SIMON: Has that got something to do with your saying there has been no theatre in the last ten years? And do you mean in America only, or in the world?

BEHRMAN: Well, to tell you the truth, I really shouldn't talk about it. I go to the theatre very little, hardly ever, and I have no impulse to go. The theatre is a highly competitive enterprise and I'm not competitive enough. Going to the theatre in New York is like mountain climbing.

SIMON: The prices are certainly steep enough.

BEHRMAN: And the theatres are hideous when you get in them. What I resent most of all is the intermissions. There you are stifled. I think it's most uncivilized—the physical aspects of the New York theatre.

SIMON: But this must have been pretty much the same thing in your youth. The real change in the theatre has been the trend away from naturalism in the writing. Is that perhaps what you object to, since your plays tend to be essentially realistic?

BEHRMAN: They are essentially realistic. I have an innate prejudice against symbolism, and I realize this is a limitation. *Waiting for Godot*, I'm told, is a great play. I don't think it is. Whom are they waiting for? Fundamentally, I resent the fact that anybody should

[42]

wait for anybody. I think that you should have a character of your own and achieve a certain independence for yourself. And most of the new plays I've seen are exercises in nullity. At least, they don't mean anything to me, which may be a sign of my age.

SIMON: Well, never mind today's avant-garde; how do you feel about the attempts of writers like Ibsen and Strindberg to get away from realism in some of their plays?

BEHRMAN: Oh well, I grew up on both and they are wonderful and great plays—

SIMON: Even the unrealistic ones, like *Brand*, for instance?

BEHRMAN: *Brand*? I didn't care much for it even when I was young. I don't think I would care for it if I read it now.

SIMON: What about *Peer Gynt*?

BEHRMAN: *Peer Gynt* enchants me. I just find it adorable, much of it. My favorite play of Ibsen's is *The Wild Duck*.

SIMON: Well, that is essentially realistic, though its overtones are symbolist.

BEHRMAN: And I love Chekhov—but shooting that gull doesn't mean much to me.

SIMON: You prefer shooting wild ducks?

BEHRMAN: I don't like mysteries. I like, in so far as one can, being clear about what one means and feels, and symbolism seems a kind of easy escape to me.

SIMON: Well, what about the kind of unreality that you get in *The Importance of Being Earnest*?

BEHRMAN: It's my favorite play. I think that's the most marvelous play in the world: it's so enchantingly funny and it's a miracle of style.

SIMON: Have you not found any recent plays, realistic or otherwise, that have pleased you? How about Albee, for example?

BEHRMAN: I think *Virginia Woolf* is a dreadful play. He's got enormous talent as a writer. He writes wonderful dialogue. He has a buttonholing quality, and he just compels us to listen. But I think it's one of the falsest and emptiest plays I've ever seen. I very much liked *The Zoo Story*, however.

SIMON: What has it got that Albee's other plays do not have for you?

BEHRMAN: It is a very lively, dialectic confrontation between the

[43]

two people. I know the people. Though the end of that, too, is meaningless.

SIMON: How about Ionesco?

BEHRMAN: I saw *Rhinoceros*, and I liked that. I liked the fact that everybody wanted to be a rhinoceros: that's one of the stigmata of our times.

SIMON: What about some of the new English dramatists?

BEHRMAN: Well, I loved *A Taste of Honey*; it's one of my favorite plays. But Osborne, for instance, I do not like at all.

SIMON: And how about Brendan Behan?

BEHRMAN: I enjoyed *The Hostage* enormously. But I didn't feel that there was a creative artist there. I felt that there was a man who managed in one evening to convey his personality and his good spirits and what tortured him, and that he'll never do anything beyond that.

SIMON: And what of the Swiss playwrights, Dürrenmatt and Frisch?

BEHRMAN: Well, I loved *The Visit*. It was wonderful, but I thought also that it was untrue. There is no community where there isn't one decent person. I do not believe in that community where everyone is an absolutely nefarious criminal or crook. If I have to believe that there's just no potentiality at all for good in humanity, then I see no point in living. God knows, I expect nothing of people. I have a very poor opinion of the human race, but what I think is remarkable is that there are occasionally marvelous individuals who behave disinterestedly and purely.

SIMON: Is that, conceivably, what lies behind your plays?

BEHRMAN: I think so. I think so. You've gotten me to something fundamental behind all my plays—just this very thing.

SIMON: Very well, let's get to the new play then. You said that you consider *But For Whom Charlie* your best, or your most serious work—I forget exactly which.

BEHRMAN: I think that in some ways it's more realistic than my other plays.

SIMON: How would you summarize the intentions in, or behind, this play?

BEHRMAN: That all that matters in life, really the ultimate thing that matters, is scrupulosity. Being scrupulous when it's difficult to be scrupulous. Undertaking the sense of responsibility.

SIMON: More than in any other play of yours, I would guess, the forces of evil are present in this one. Sexual hostilities or threats are consummated here; basically bad people are much more in evidence than before. What are you trying to say about evil?

BEHRMAN: That it works in the world, and, as one of my characters says in one place of evil men and women, "They possess the earth." But also that there's a counterforce of conscience and purity which is expressed by Seymour, which cannot be discounted either. It will count as long as there's any civilization worth considering at all. And it cannot be discounted that power, strength, is not a monopoly of evil.

SIMON: And what does the joint departure of Charlie and Gillian in the end mean?

BEHRMAN: It means a good time, that's all. But they'll also have plenty of trouble.

SIMON: That, perhaps, they're being punished by their very association?

BEHRMAN: Yes. They're deserving of each other. The important thing is that at the end Seymour is helping a helpless artist and is sticking to it.

SIMON: I'm a bit sorry that that artist, Sheila, gets so little to do in the play. I'm not sure that from that very brief scene at the end the image of what she stands for emerges.

BEHRMAN: I may tell you that at one time I wanted to call the play *Sheila and the Saints.* Don't you think that's a nice title? They wouldn't accept it. But in the first act Seymour talks about her and says, "She's interested in sainthood." I hope that'll remain with the audience after that vast stretch of time.

SIMON: Did you find this play easier or harder to write than the others?

BEHRMAN: Easier. I carried that idea around for very many years. My first notes on it were taken thirteen years ago. But when I got to write it, I just couldn't stop and wrote it really very quickly. The first act was at once accepted.

SIMON: I can see that several of the characters must have real-life analogues, but I'm curious whether someone as good as Seymour

Rosenthal ever really runs a foundation. Is there a real-life
Seymour?

BEHRMAN: Well, I'm not sure either, but conceivably he might.

SIMON: In other words, he is not a real person?

BEHRMAN: No. Gillian and Charlie are, but I don't think I know a
Seymour.

SIMON: I was afraid of that. But I am delighted to note than in many
of your plays, as in this one, music plays maybe not a prominent
but a charming subsidiary role. And it's interesting that it's always Bach or Brahms or Schubert as in *No Time for Comedy*.

BEHRMAN: And Strauss. I had him in *The Second Man*. The *Rosen-
kavalier* waltz. In 1927 it wasn't the cliché it is now.

SIMON: But it's always conservative music. The only time that a
"modernist" composer is mentioned, it is Shostakovich, and I
notice that his name is misspelled.

BEHRMAN: In *Rain From Heaven*. Oh, that's very funny. Well, I had
a passion for music all my life and tried to study the piano and
never could. Even when I went to Hollywood I got a piano
teacher and I had to travel all the way out to her. It's what I
really would have liked to devote my life to. But I grew up on
all the classical composers. You have to hear with new ears to
hear those other people. I was a friend of Schoenberg's in Hollywood, but never understood him.

SIMON: Well, the music you like fits in with the gentle and at the
same time orderly writing you practice. Are you also interested
in the plastic arts?

BEHRMAN: I don't know anything about them. When the project to
write about Duveen came up, I said to Shawn of *The New Yorker*,
"I can't do it. I don't know anything about painting." Fortu-
nately, I found out that Duveen didn't either, so it was all right.
So the book is really a study of commerce and of a personality.

SIMON: Well, after literature, what would you name as your main
interest?

BEHRMAN: *Ahead* of literature, music. I really love music. At night
I play the radio and listen to music. I don't go to concerts any
more, but I used to hear every one of them. To a lesser degree,
I was also an opera fan. As for the plastic arts, I merely read about

them because I feel I should. I know Harold Rosenberg is considered good, but I am always awfully happy when I finish one of his articles.

SIMON: Since you're going to devote yourself to fiction now, who are some of the novelists you admire?

BEHRMAN: I'm not very well read, you know. I think Evelyn Waugh is great. He's a monster as a person. I have met him and couldn't endure him, but he's a marvelous writer. And I like Conrad very much. I know he's kind of old hat, but I like him.

SIMON: One last question. Where do you stand on movies? Not the Hollywood kind, but film as an art form?

BEHRMAN: I haven't gone to the movies in years. You see, I've worked on so many pictures of the Hollywood type, and I know that they go on long after they should end, and I've spent so much time in the projection rooms that I just don't go. I know that there are wonderful things being done now by new people, but I'd rather read in the evening, and I just am not qualified to say.

SIMON: Have you any other hobbies we should mention?

BEHRMAN: I really don't have any. At night I read.

"*What goes into creative acts is not always apparent at the moment of their performance.*" From left to right, Arthur Miller, Elia Kazan, Robert Whitehead.

A Theatre: Heart and Mind
by Barry Hyams

A PERMANENT REPERTORY COMPANY is Theatre in the most civilized degree. It is a grouping of living cells interacting to create a
higher form of life. It is an idea; yet it is empiric. It is in continuous
evolution; still it is constant. There is nothing abstract in its function;
its separate parts are people and its existence is in their singleness. It is
not noteworthy as a hardy species; yet it persists. This century has
brought forth three. The Civic Repertory of the 20's, evanescent as
it was, proved the most durable. The Repertory Theater of Lincoln
Center is the fourth.

The resolve to be born had thrust upon the Repertory Theater
the burden of public trust and expectancy. It might have gestated in
a quiet retreat but for its directors and their persuasion that a repertory
company was not a private endeavor, inspired in solitude perhaps, but
engaging the public from the moment of conception. In isolation it
could not recapture the dignity of the theatre. Theatre and audience
were a symbiosis, growing together in open air and light. Only in
performance could it certify the mutual faith between the artist and
the community.

The Repertory Theater of Lincoln Center became the child of
Elia Kazan and Robert Whitehead. During their years of contemplation and exploration, director and producer fused into one. Their collaboration was a synthesis of experience and dreams. They examined
the great theatres of Europe, traveling there, and later throughout
America to cull young and veteran talent. They drew to them artists
who shared their vision, who were moved by the dithyrambs of yore

[49]

and today, to whom the theatre was a source of divine intoxication, and they shaped their vision in a physical structure and in an ensemble of playwrights, actors, directors and designers.

Robert Whitehead lived longest with the Repertory Theater dream. As consultant to Lincoln Center, he generated a climate of adventure, acting as steel upon the flint of Elia Kazan, together igniting Eero Saarinen and Jo Mielziner, the designers of the Vivian Beaumont Theater at the Center. They also sparked Arthur Miller and S. N. Behrman, José Quintero and David Hays. All approached the experience in a spirit of initiation. To all it presented a curious twin sensation: the excitement of anticipation and the tremblings of approaching fulfillment. Each from his own perspective prepared to face the new view. Each spoke with his innermost voice. In the beginning was the idea; and to begin with, Whitehead reflected upon how it was made tangible.

The ANTA Washington Square Theatre resulted from Model O. There was, therefore, Model A, B, C, D and so on. Each of these models seemed to represent the solution, but each provoked further ideas and discussion which were resolved in another refinement. The greatest credit must go to Eero Saarinen and Jo Mielziner for bringing us at last to Models M and N and finally to "O," which is at present under construction at Lincoln Center as the Vivian Beaumont Theater. The ANTA Washington Square Theatre is a close approximation of that same form, particularly in the relationship of the audience to the actor.

The talking began about five years ago. We did not set out to design an open stage or a proscenium stage, a Greek amphitheatre or an Elizabethan stage. Though the ultimate form was the result of many influences, it simply evolved. We talked about plays, playwrights and themes, about plays and productions that had meant something to us and had conditioned the growth of our theatre in this country. We designed models for various plays. I particularly remember the models for *Death of a Salesman* and *The Emperor Jones*. We examined a hypothetical actor at a certain point and asked, "Where are the seats in relation to him and in relation to what we want a particular play to express?" In determining this the stage began to move out into the audience. There was, at first, a proscenium, a ramp on either side of it and a considerable apron; but as we discussed additional plays, productions and ideas, the actor and his environment were gradually drawn more and more into the room with the audience and the more that happened, the more the proscenium moved out of focus. I remember at the time of these discussions I was also planning the production of *A Man For All Seasons*, a play that dealt with man's conscience and the law. Could it be more effective if that argument took place in the same room with its audience? It seemed it could. The staircase in the setting could sweep right out into the house. It was totally arbitrary. People went upstairs to dinner, to bed, to the river, anywhere desired. The stairs had no architectural meaning. They were designed to serve poetic theatricality with greater strength. The effort to attain theatricality with greater strength was what eventually brought us to Model O. Actually its form had no precise precedent in this country or elsewhere though many of its elements existed in Stratford, Ontario, in Chichester, England, the Tyrone Guthrie Theatre in Minneapolis, the Loeb Theatre in Cambridge, Massachusetts, and the classic Greek and Roman theatres.

Elia Kazan and I spoke with many writers who, we hoped, would create plays for this theatre. Arthur Miller and S. N. Behrman were among the first to commit their work to us. We had always wished to have our opening season composed entirely of American plays. That Eugene O'Neill be represented was and is of great importance to the theatre's purpose. The visual eloquence of *Marco Millions* seemed to fit effectively between *After The Fall* and *But For Whom Charlie*, and perhaps more importantly all three expressed in their content a common intention. They asked that we look at ourselves and at the world all of us have created. This intention, whether it be in terms of comedy, drama or tragedy, will be rooted in every play this theatre produces.

The company, as it exists at this moment, was born out of this season's production needs and next season's ideas. We sought people who were not only talented actors, but who, we felt, were equipped as human beings to help in this kind of movement. There are actors who are not with us who, we wish, were. New people will enter over

[51]

the years; others after spending two or more seasons with us possibly may leave. It will take some years to build the company, time, trial and error to achieve an ensemble whose members, wherever they may be, will be identified with the character of this repertory.

A serious theatre company designed to function on a permanent basis would be inconceivable without a rigorous training program—more precisely, an academy with a three-to-four year curriculum attached and organically related to the life of that theatre. Such a school is being planned by Juilliard, the educational wing of Lincoln Center for the Performing Arts, and must be a source from which our theatre will derive strength.

And so, the last five years have been spent working with ideas, architects and designer, with writers and actors and with a number of our most enlightened business leaders, all of whom contributed to making the Repertory Theater possible, to clearing the ground upon which it could be founded. I do not think these steps could have been taken thirty years ago. I do not think it happened at this time because John D. Rockefeller and his associates came together, nor because they brought us together. With all the good will in the world it could not have come about without the atmosphere that currently exists in the nation. We have reached a point in our history—possibly it is a maturity; certainly it is a psychology, a need that exists and that has already made possible such outbursts of community activity as exhibited in Washington, Minneapolis, San Francisco, Seattle, Houston, Stratford, Connecticut and Stratford, Ontario. There are reputedly some sixty-eight centers of music and theatre that are in the process of being born in various parts of this nation. Economic conditions have reduced the volume of theatre production in New York below what it was when the population was considerably smaller; but the talent and vigor of our expanding population has burst out in many areas. Lincoln Center is one manifestation; and Lincoln Center being in New York City has the professional possibility of being most fully realized if the job is done properly.

This season we are doing three plays. In the years to come, we will do more—works of European writers from all periods of theatre literature, plays of American writers, new and old. Whatever plays they may be, whether they deal with history, whether they be new or classic, they must be produced through our view of our own time. If the hopes and experiences of our lives are expressed through the work that is produced in this theatre, a common and lasting relationship with its audience can be built. Ultimately something may be achieved to which the audience, that is to say, the people of this country, may look with a sense of personal possession and pride.

Working with Eero Saarinen, Jo Mielziner regarded the Vivian Beaumont Theater not as an end in itself nor as an abstraction. It was to incorporate the most advanced facilities that funds, design and craftsmanship could provide. It was to function also as a challenge to those who were to work in it. Unable to wait until 1965 and the completion of the Vivian Beaumont at Lincoln Center, the directors of the Repertory Theater instigated on the campus of New York University the construction of an interim home, a playhouse parallel in form to the one being erected uptown. Exigent factors made the resulting ANTA Washington Square Theatre subject to limitations. Precedent, novelty and arbitrariness were at his elbow as Mielziner fashioned its interior.

This theatre was born out of necessity. During the thirteen months of working on the ANTA Washington Square home for the Repertory Theater, I really tried to think and work not as a scene designer, not as a man interested in theatre architecture, but as a member of a creative team that is devoted to the idea of a repertory company in New York. And, particularly, for Lincoln Center.

The major problem was basically time and budgetary limitations. A year is precious little for designing a theatre, much less getting it built and opened. A good theatre should be on the drafting board and in the minds of the ultimate users of the theatre literally for a couple of years. We had to make these decisions in weeks and to accept the fact that this was a temporary structure and, therefore, the materials would not be ideal. The shape of the auditorium would not be sacrificed; it had to be as favorable as possible for the relationship between the stage, the actor and the audience. The means given to the director and the actor and the scenic problems had to be reduced to

[53]

the simplest terms. We eliminated the traditional fly loft of the stage-house. The back-stage was uncomfortably and frighteningly small. The same is true of the secondary elements for the audience. Lobby space, toilet facilities, entrances, box-office space, all were cut to the bone because there had to be 1100 seats and all those seats had to be well situated for the full enjoyment of the play.

I have seldom seen a setting used in a repertory company that would be ideal if you were doing it for a single specific production. Usually a repertory company has to utilize scenic and lighting facilities in terms of their partial use for one production and their eventual use, perhaps, in a dozen others. The same was true here. We had to devise means that were so simple that a freshness in imagination and a newness in the technical approach would compensate for the variety normally available. All past repertory theatres represented precedents. Yet, in this case, even a repertory theatre's generous back-stage was absent. The back-stage of a repertory usually has eight-to-ten times the working area of the conventional American theatre. Because of the need to store productions, the average European repertory theatre building uses about one-tenth of its space as playing area; the rest is live storage and rehearsal space. ANTA Washington Square had room for none of this.

Limitations are often frightening but never serious if you have courage and if you hit hard with the things that count and give up the things that are secondary. We were giving up a lot of things that were regarded as precious. I used to think that to bring a house curtain down on a scene was absolutely necessary. We did not have any curtain on this stage. We had neither the space to draw it off-stage, nor a stage-house to fly it. So we would do things with lights we thought would be acceptable. They would be acceptable if we did them well. That is one of the qualities about repertory; it's what you do well, so well that the things you give up are soon noticed neither by the public nor by the artist back-stage.

Our thrust stage is very close in area and not unlike the shape of the Repertory's eventual home. The back-stage area of the Vivian Beaumont Theater will be over twenty-five times the size of the back-stage at the ANTA Washington Square. Downtown we have mainly to work scenically with the most fluent element at the designer's disposal, that is, stage lighting. We have good equipment and, I hope, creative imaginative lighting. The rafters, exposed dark factory trusses of steel hung over the audience's head, are our light pipes on which hang the lighting equipment without masking of any sort. We make no secret of what we need to light our productions. Our thrust stage has a variety of levels and forms. The designers collaborated and agreed on what was acceptable to the directors of the respective plays. We could not hang scenery; we could draw no curtains; so we created a simple set of screens made of fire-proof woven wood, that hung on tracks and that pushed on- and off-stage.

Both the ANTA Washington Square and the Vivian Beaumont are based on the desired relationship between the acting area and the viewing area. There are many theatres throughout the world built with a thrust stage. Our seating plan is not original. It is as old and tried as the Greek and Roman theatres with their steeply banked rows of seats. Their seating capacity was much larger than ours because their stylization was such that words were almost chanted and shouted and sung. Gestures were choreographic. In fact, the whole scale, visually and orally, was different. If we were building a musical house, we could go beyond a 65-foot to 100- and 150-foot distance between the last rows and the stage. In planning the seating arrangements, it was our thought to get as many seats as possible as close to the stage as possible. At a 100-foot distance, an actress with good lungs can be heard, and possibly her facial expressions can be seen. You know she has a nose and you see a mouth and eyes, but all subtlety of expression is lost when you are far beyond 65 feet. Similar to the Vivian Beaumont, the seats at the ANTA Washington Square are all within 65 feet of the playing area, within intimate range. Luxurious leg room for each seat would have been a nice addendum to the pleasure of play-going but comfort itself had to bow to that indispensable need for actor-audience relationship. Luxury of seating ends up in forcing about half of the audience to a point too distant for the full enjoyment of a vital performance.

For the Vivian Beaumont we had both the time and the funds to study materials. We wouldn't think of having exposed metal beams there; although it, too, will be a functional theatre. In neither theatre did we have a sense of creating an auditorium, a décor by itself. ANTA

Washington Square is reduced to near austerity. There is carpet on stairs up and down the steeply banked aisles. The seats are upholstered. We have air-conditioning, and heating on a cold night. There is enough light in the intermission to read a program. But there is no décor. The scenes and acts are not punctuated by the closing of a curtain. This is done with lights. If we have been bold about it, if we are convinced that it is good, the audience will be convinced as we are.

Toward the end of the Renaissance, the Greek and Roman amphitheatres were forgotten. The 17th, 18th and early 19th Century theatres were influenced more by court-life and how His Highness and Her Royal Majesty could be entertained. That is why the side seats in those theatres face the Royal Box rather than the stage; it was more important to see how the King was reacting to a scene than how the player was acting for the audience. That kind of opera house lived for many centuries and is still unfortunately reflected in some architectural designs today.

The physical traits of a theatre determine its style of production. In the crudest sense, a vast auditorium will preclude intimacy; a small theatre will nullify spectacle. Size and surroundings exert subtle influences also on the playwright and his approach to his audience, bounding or liberating substance and form, expanding or shrinking his perspective, even toward the familiar. The prospect of the new structure and its housing of a permanent acting company afforded Arthur Miller a look rearward and ahead, a re-examination of the interdependence of theatre artists and their alliance with the audience.

The ideal theatre design would provide great intimacy without becoming, in effect, somebody's living room, and the whole thing squirming in the audience's lap. That leads to naturalistic acting because the actor need not project himself, and it ultimately encourages naturalistic writing. The audience must not be in a relationship of such intimacy to the play as to thwart a reach toward poetry or austerity. I wanted, if possible, a theatre where you could create a very minute and intimate effect or, equally, one of great size, even a classical effect,

[56]

the opposite of naturalistic intimacy. I've seen many designs for theatres, and there is no one design that will do both well at the same time. It seems to me the design we have is probably as close as you can get to it: a stage that juts out to the audience but has tremendous depth from the forward edge of the stage to the back wall, with possibilities of extraordinary elongation so that as you recede from the audience you must become larger than life, while at the front of the stage, the effect of a close-up lens is possible.

I have not been accustomed to thinking architecturally. It was never asked of me. On Broadway, you take what you get. It became an issue for me while writing this play. If it is to be fully effective, it must sometimes change within a split second from the most intimate feeling to the most social and abstract feeling, in an attempt to fill the gap between the two with human feeling. I began to think in terms of an architecture that would make that possible. In effect, *After The Fall* has called for a certain kind of flexible theatre beyond the scope of the proscenium design. And I don't know of a better kind than this theatre and this design.

Originally, when I started to write the play, I didn't think we were actually going to build a theatre to accommodate a play. It is not often that possibility arises. The first thought was that we could somehow adapt an existing armory and build into it such a design; or, if we were forced into a Broadway theatre, we would build the stage out toward the audience. That would have created a problem of reducing the number of seats. When the possibility arose actually to erect a theatre, this whole thing took on a reality and the theatre was built around the need which the script created.

A theatre design of itself will not revolutionize playwrighting. If a real-estate entrepreneur saw fit to build a new theatre and constructed exactly the one we have built, it probably wouldn't inspire playwrights directly to a different kind of drama. Possibly, it might stimulate more amplitude. But I can't separate this theatre from the whole concept of repertory and a permanent company. That does effect a change, a simple and direct change. The commercial theatre has always boasted, as have those who have succeeded in it, that they could make do, let's say, with two actors instead of ten, and that this was a virtue of the Broadway theatre, that we were experts at doing things for the minimum economic cost in terms of actors and so on. I never saw the virtue in it. Many great plays require, quite simply, a crowd of people. *Oedipus* is one of them. Almost any Greek play requires a chorus. Well, a chorus has to be good or it is not a good chorus. That means good actors, trained to be a chorus, rehearsed as accurately as leading characters have to be. That could not be done readily in the Broadway theatre because of the salaries entailed, and if the management skimped and hired untrained actors or those who would work for less because they lacked experience, the result would be a worse chorus, or a crowd that was inept, and an inept crowd can be as damaging to a play as an inept leading man. With the Repertory, and in this theatre, images can be called up requiring as much expertness as the leading role and can be used importantly, something I would be loth to do in the face of the hard stare of Broadway's economic situation. A great play or a good play does not necessarily have to fill the house every night, but a play that does not fill the house every night does not exist on Broadway, cannot exist, and it is nobody's individual fault. It is just the real-estate situation, the tax situation, and the rest of it. This lays an artificial burden on playwrighting and there is no virtue anymore in saying one has overcome this because it means in being denied legs one has learned to crawl gracefully.

In this Repertory Theater, I can use leading actors in important roles that are not leading roles so that the whole play can take on the size, the amplitude it originally had in my vision. On Broadway it gets reduced, and one begins inevitably to make a virtue of expedients. It isn't a question whether it is Eugene O'Neill or me or Tennessee Williams or anybody else; you face the existing situation. People have forgotten that Ibsen and Strindberg and others wrote in repertory theatres where they had the advantage of this kind of freedom and that for one thing, their plays in many cases lasted four hours with complex, full-blown developments of story and theme. They were not accommodating an after-theatre train schedule to Westport and then were criticized for writing small works. A large canvas is needed for large works and now we have a large canvas. It is a great challenge to playwrights and now they have no one to blame but themselves if they do not meet it.

There are plays that require more than two-and-a-half weeks

rehearsal. With others, if you took more than two-and-a-half weeks, you wouldn't know what to do with the time. But any play of a certain density, of a certain complexity, of a certain breadth, cannot be done properly in two-and-a-half weeks. There is no way to do it. Once you have the spread of three months we have, there suddenly open up vistas within the play that neither the directors nor the actors are accustomed to exploring. For the first time in all my years in the theatre, I read the play to the actors, who, until then, had not heard the complete work. This had never been done because nobody would take that vital time out of two-and-a-half weeks since every day, every hour is decisive. Not that I am a better actor, but reading it, I put into the play the tonalities, the meanings, the shadings that in this case took two years of writing to achieve. The actors were surprised by these implications. Inevitably, when an actor picks up a play he reads it once looking for his role because that is what he will be required to do in it. This time he sat back and listened to the whole story and saw where he fit into it. My reading it gave them a sense of the whole arc of the play.

Another thing, never to my knowledge done on Broadway, was the next step. The actors read and I at any point interjected a comment. I could hear by the way the actor was reading the line that he was not yet acting but I sensed his intention or confusion about the line. I gave him what I knew about this line. The director at times was surprised to see that he had not understood exactly what I'd meant. So we got into a three-way discussion, and, in some cases, went on for ten minutes about one phrase, in terms of its connection backward and forward in the play. Suddenly the light dawned on the actor who had been playing or thinking about a line or scene. He saw this line or scene was not there just to make its effect of the moment but that it was the interaction of three other thoughts that had occurred before on page 12, page 19 and page 44, and finally, in full form on page 98. In this way, I gave him the inner connections which took me so long to discover myself.

This was not taking place in some office with the leading man and the leading lady. The secondary, smaller roles were in on this whole discussion, so that each person knew what the implications were of his action on the whole, on the largest level, on the largest canvas. And the importance of his role began to occur to him. Even the smallest one said, "My God, if I am not there, and I don't do this right, it is not simply that I haven't done some small thing right, but that I have prevented the next great step from being taken." Presumably a well-written play has no roles that don't matter.

It is hard to say what effect this theatre will have on the future in respect to style or form. I can't speak for any other writer. For myself, it would guarantee for me the continuation of the adventure of playwrighting. *After The Fall* is experimental in any terms. It involves what is not a new theatrical style so much as a new style of thinking about the world, the unification, the synthesis of individual psychology and social and moral considerations to make a moral biology on the stage. Instead of having a work concentrate on one element of man, I have tried to put him on in totality. And, that adventure is endless because if that finally becomes the aim, there will always be a new way to do it.

This freedom presents the challenge of the theatre. I have met the other challenges. I can construct a play and make one that meets the demands of the theatre we have had. We have had plays that are a personal statement but have a very narrow compass, no general statement, because they are so personal. We have had, in the past, one or the other. I connect this, and I think rightly, with the nature of the theatre as it was. The Repertory Theater is a public theatre. It no longer is a luxurious little by-way of existence for a few people who are perhaps connoisseurs, or for one reason or another are interested in somebody's personal statement. This is now in effect supported by the population at large. It has to face them just as every great theatre in the past did. The closet drama has its virtues but we never connect it with any statement of breadth. At best, it makes a comment about human behavior in a specific circumstance and is limited by that circumstance. Where the great theatres came in Greece and in Elizabethan times, it was to the widest mass that the statement was made and, to make its effect, had to be both most specific and most general. Nothing was taken for granted, nothing, in the sense that this was a clique with an inside view of life and that the playwright represented some previously accepted standard that everybody in this clique shared consciously or unconsciously. The big drama in the big theatres was always shared with the population at large, with all that mixture of standards involved in facing that population. We haven't done that yet. As time goes by I hope we will. It requires the widest stretch of imagination and the widest stretch of effort to face that audience, and we now have a physical plant in which to do it, the seed of a fine company, and above all, a fertile viewpoint.

So many forces in this kind of theatre press toward a more ample vision: for example, first-class leading actors will sometimes play important but not principal roles. This fairly invites the reaching out beyond a single line of development in a play to a much wider embrace of life, when a relatively minor but important character may be quickly developed, set on the stage and related to the story without being regarded as an unnecessary side development. A man in this play has to talk to somebody and give the effect of a realistic character in a realistic conversation. In the middle of a speech, he must move out of that realistic matrix and expand it to its generalized significance. But, he cannot do this as though he had walked into that theatre from 45th Street. It must be clear to the audience that he is acting, but not imitating; in a word, he must carry the audience through its passion for identification and into a passion for knowing. And we are not prepared to do that yet; we have not had that kind of acting because we have no classical repertory; and actors recognize that they have to expand their own awareness and their own talent to encompass this kind of technique. It is still based upon psychological truth and so on, but the style is very much different; it is no mere imitation of "life."

A by-no-means-exact analogy is when an Elizabethan actor carries on a passionate scene with another and that scene sharply turns into a soliloquy. The passion of the soliloquy is of a different kind because it is the passion of awareness. We have not been able to jump in our American realistic theatre to that passion of awareness without losing psychological reality. I have felt for years a boredom with the theatre of tears and laughter. There is a limit to such passions if the mind is blocked out, a limit of interest and finally an untruthfulness. All I am trying to do in this theatre is to bring the mind back so as to make real on stage as in life that part of man which, through passion, seeks awareness. There is no contradiction between the two.

[61]

Action and word are not always compatible on stage. One may illumine the other or at times one may blur the other. The sine qua non *of a theatre is that it aid the actor in transmitting both with clarity to the audience. Granted this cooperation the dramatist if so inclined is then unmuzzled, freed to convey whatever is dependent upon words. In the new theatre, S. N. Behrman found the promise of this collaboration an immediate and heartening aspect.*

When I walked into the ANTA Washington Square Theatre I was staggered by what I saw. The austerity of the beams, of the walls, had a spare, Puritanic beauty. I welcomed the absence of frill. Everything seemed to be there for the purpose of sitting down and seeing a play. I saw the apron jutting out into the audience and I was excited and moved when I thought of *But For Whom Charlie* in relation to it.

My plays are dependent, from the very beginning, not on effects, not on melodrama. They are verbal plays. That is why I required a certain kind of actor. I required actors like the Lunts, Ina Claire, like Laurence Olivier, who could speak English in a certain way. If you miss the verbal qualities in my plays, you miss a great deal, what otherwise you might not miss at all in plays where meaning is revealed without words, conveyed through action. In the case of *But For Whom Charlie* I felt a thrill of anticipation because the quality of the play, the shadings of meaning, the kind that come from words, from the inflections and from the emphasis would be there for the audience and would not be missed.

I have had over and over again experiences in the theatre where either because the actors were not aware of the implications of certain lines or because of the size of the theatres in which they appeared, the things most precious to me as a writer vanished, did not emerge. Here the play would stand or fall for what it was. I would not be able to blame anyone because everything that was in the play would be audible and the audience would participate in the conversation that would take place on the stage. You cannot shout a conversation. What I want is audibility without volume, and I felt I would get that in this theatre.

Some of my plays have been performed in very deep theatres. My first play, *The Second Man,* was done in London. On a Saturday night I went up to the second balcony. The house was full. Where I had stood downstairs the audience was laughing, but when I went up to the balcony the audience was not laughing because they could not hear. They only heard lines that were spoken for big effect. They did not hear the minutiae of the dialogue. I had hoped that whatever would be spoken, the audience would be right there to respond if they wanted to. Of course, I do not wish audiences literally to reply; the answers I write are more apt than the audience could improvise.

Max Beerbohm in *Around Theatres* once described seeing a play from the "pit," an occasion brought about by a leading actor denying the critic his accustomed stall seats.

> . . . *He no longer wanted my hints on the art of acting, and so, as a hint on the art of criticism, he ceased to send me tickets for his theatre.*
>
> *Not until I was seated did I realize that the play had begun. I listened intently. I strained my ears. Certainly, Mr. Arthur Bourchier, Miss Vanbrugh, Mr. Aubrey Smith and other persons engaged in* The Fascinating Mr. Vanderveldt (*by Alfred Sutro*) *are not bad elocutionists. And yet with all my attention, I was constantly failing to overhear them and having to use my experience of plays in general as a means of guessing a drift. I saw Miss Vanbrugh cross the stage and lay her hands in the hands of another lady. And I heard this sound: Want—pew. From the context of the play and from the deportment of the two actresses, I was able to guess that Miss Vanbrugh had said, "I want to help you."*
>
> *I begin to understand why there is so little demand for dramatic truth to life. The majority of people going to the play know that they cannot see anything that will remind them of actual life. What matter, then, how great be the degree of remoteness from reality?*
>
> *The marvel to me since my visit to the pit of the Garrick Theatre is not that the public cares so little for dramatic truth but that it can sometimes tolerate a play which is not either the wildest melodrama or the wildest farce. Where low tones and fine shades are practically invisible one would expect an exclusive insistence on splodges of garish color . . .*

(Around Theatres: *In the Pit, May 12, 1906*)

As a result of knowing the architecture of the ANTA Washington Square Theatre and having the setting described to me, an abstract set such as I have never used in my life, it was possible for me to write this play with much greater freedom than ever before. And this play requires what this stage gives it. Formerly when I needed a staircase, there was an elaborate staircase. Here, we just threw up a staircase—only five or six steps on it—and it provides an entire playing area I never pictured when I first wrote the play. It lends different intensities in the character relationships. Its height is realism, an intensification of realism through the imagination, which is the ultimate of realism.

Many an actor, unaccustomed to the peninsula stage, finds himself hurled by it into strange propinquity with the audience. Gone is the familiar "fourth wall," once a barrier between player and viewer, now no longer available as a haven from distracting proximity. The ANTA Washington Square Theatre is kin but not identical to the condition of the arena stage. José Quintero, intimate of the proscenium and in-the-round theatres, has directed in both and has contended with the virtues and hazards their space relationships present to actor and audience.

Theatre-in-the-round has its stage in the center of the arena surrounded on all sides by the audience. The Repertory Theater stage is three-sided. It is not new nor is its increasing popularity due to economy of production. The reason is that we have become interested in the individual character rather than in having him submerged and reduced by pretty pictures. Even in the proscenium theatre, the playwright and the designer who serves his needs have thrust part of the set into the audience and dispensed with the curtain. In *Cat On A Hot Tin Roof*, Jo Mielziner designed a platform to project beyond the proscenium because Tennessee Williams had written long subjective monologues and Elia Kazan, directing the play, must have felt the need for the audience to know with more immediacy that what that girl was saying was coming from deep inside her and therefore had to be viewed from close up.

The most important things is that this theatre, as a physical structure, is flexible enough to accommodate the demands of any play.

[64]

"*Every play has a different kind of reality. Whatever its reality, it has to be performed on this stage more intensely, with greater subtlety.*"
—José Quintero

Most of the time, the only element in a production that is not flexible to the environment and reality of a play is the theatre itself. A director has to live within the play's environment. The actor is subjugated by his role, the designer by the milieu. But for the most part, the theatre remains absolutely immobile. It does not move. The proscenium theatre provides one frame and regardless of the play's needs it does not change. ANTA Washington Square combines the proscenium theatre with the virtues of what is called theatre-in-the-round, or more exactly, the Greek theatre and Shakespearean theatre. It affords a flexibility that will serve the needs of a play that much more.

In an open theatre where you can dictate the way your actor moves, you can determine the shape and form of the stage. The Repertory Theater has an enormous, round "apron." It may be made into a square by the simple device of platforms. It could be made triangular so that it becomes a flat pyramid projecting into the audience. This theatre can change and a director may have a great deal to do with changing its shape because its openness supplies elasticity and an intimacy with the audience that is not present with a proscenium. Thornton Wilder said, talking about how much he preferred a three-quarter stage, that the conventional stage was like a woman in Paris who went to see *Camille* and wept and wept at the death of Camille while her chauffeur froze to death outside. The proscenium stage imposes a division, an unreality of much less identification, all identification possessing different qualities. In-the-round, just by the physical proximity of the players to the audience, forces a new sense of identification, a new texture of identification.

Disadvantages? I cannot see any because at the Repertory Theater you may still stage a pageant within a frame. Its absence doesn't deprive us of a proscenium altogether. The rear of the stage may be treated as if one were working in a proscenium where movement is linear. When the actor takes his position on the apron, movement becomes curved. An actor who has always played on the proscenium stage is terrified the first time he plays in-the-round or three-quarter. He has learned a technique in the proscenium that is not valid in-the-round such as upstage being the most favorable position. In-the-round does not have an upstage or downstage in terms of importance of area. An actor whose instinct has not been trained in that technique finds the emotional salience of in-the-round incomprehensible and it throws him. It also breaks one of the proscenium rules. How often has an actor complained of a director facing him upstage in the most crucial scene in the play? In-the-round, his back is always to one part of the audience. Thereupon the actor must begin to realize that his whole body is a transmitter, a sculptural concept on stage in contrast with a flat painting. This demands techniques from actors such as the freedom to move without restriction, to use his back, his profile, his whole figure, and to recognize himself as a total person rather than a two-dimensional one.

But the problem for the actor is deeper and lies in the intimacy of the thrust theatre. The audience is all around him and very close. Where formerly he could produce certain effects in the proscenium theatre, he no longer has the same space between him and the audience. Therefore, he is forced to a deeper kind of reality in his playing.

In directing a play for the open stage, what must be avoided is blocking the view of some portion of the audience. One must be inventive to keep the play mobile, almost as if it were a "figure eight," without the movement being unmotivated or capricious. Certain areas in view of the entire audience assume varying values, such as the farthest section. One makes the initial statement back there and then breaks it down into its components down center.

The further away, the more general is the view. The closer to the audience, the fewer get a frontal view, but get some profile of the subject. For that reason, a general statement is more removed and particulars are close up. Not that particulars are less important; they are more intimate, like the pieces of a puzzle. In *Marco Millions*, the procession in the prologue starts in full view at the rear so that everyone gets the whole picture. As it passes down front, some see backs, some profiles, some full faces. Each sees a different and changing angle, and it becomes more individual because no one sees the whole anymore, only the specific from his particular angle, and each reaction to what is taking place becomes personal.

Every play has a different kind of reality. But whatever its reality, it has to be performed on this stage more intensely, with greater subtlety. It cannot be elongated and distorted for the purpose of projection. Even vocal projection is entirely different on the open

stage from a proscenium where it is sent straight out. Here the voice
has to go round and round in waves instead of being flat and linear.
Direct communication between the actor and the audience has generally been face to face; now it has to be communicated with all parts
of the body as well as the voice. Nothing can be hidden from the
audience in this intimacy. If the audience has a full view of the actor
at one time or another it will see everything about him, while in the
proscenium he can always conceal a part of himself. The thrust stage
will reveal far more than the proscenium where distance lends illusion.
Proximity to an audience denies the use of exaggerated make-up.
Deprived of the tools of concealment, the body reveals more and some
other means for illusion is found.

*Emerging from behind the proscenium onto the unprotected forestage was a
deliverance of the designer from the conventional use of scenery. To Jo
Mielziner the new theatre offered excitement in a fresh approach to fundamental problems. The elements at hand were the same; their use was to be
spare though the space was increased. It presented a new discipline.*

I have been associated with Lincoln Center for almost five years, but
I think of myself as a worker in repertory, not as a designer. I don't
think of my own little picture postcards to be done back of a single
production. I think what will happen when we do the Behrman play;
will these steps be easily moved when we do the O'Neill play? I am
part of the whole spirit of the group. I have had to think not only of
After The Fall and *But For Whom Charlie* and *Marco Millions*, but of
the unknown fourth, fifth and sixth productions, whatever they
may be.

Because of the limitation of techniques available at the ANTA
Washington Square Theatre, there is more dependence on light,
props and costumes and the very simple use of permanent screens,
painted a single color, that move on curved tracks. They can move
only in one direction, although there are three sets of them. There are
slight variations in heights and shapes of levels on the forward stage
that juts out into the audience and where the main action plays. That
is the first limitation to confront a designer.

"I don't think of little picture postcards in back of a single production but as a worker in repertory." Design: After The Fall *by Jo Mielziner.*

The second is something that is new to most of us in the American theatre. This technique of a thrust stage means that the director choreographs his actors in depth as opposed to the on-and-off stage movement of the average box set which is shallow and very wide, averaging forty feet at the proscenium, and where actors make entrances mostly from the side, occasionally from upstage or on a flat diagonal, but never from great depth. Conventional stages do not have depth because the sight lines do not permit it. The Repertory Theater stage captures the idea of working in depth. The ANTA Washington Square Theatre is almost 42 feet from the downstage position of the thrust to the furthest screen which provides our meager little backstage crossover and storage area. We also have exciting sets of levels normally not present, from the zero area at the foot of the first row of the audience to two- and three-foot elevations on the thrust, and as high as 15 or 16 feet in the air for those in the rear, giving additional dimensions in height and depth for a director's imagination. In certain plays, it will be marvelous; in others, it will have to be negated in favor of a more simple technique which is also available. When we close our downstage panel we can have a setting as little as 15 or 20 feet in depth. At the Vivian Beaumont it will be greater. Sets could be as much as 50 or 80 feet deep. It is doubtful that they will be. The far depths in the uptown theatre are designed for live storage of the productions. If we had started with fabulous facilities, if the ANTA Washington Square Theatre had been built with a 50-foot deep stage-house and a 110-foot grid height, it might have been unfavorable because the temptation to overuse scenery would have been a strong one. Instead, this theatre project has begun in the spirit of collaboration, the spirit of repertory, with the designer opening the ring to join hands with the director and the actors, all sharing in the community effort, which will be different from using the clichés, the conventional and safe media that have been at our disposal these many years.

Studying the question of lighting, I was amazed to find that the total area in which the director works is about twice that of the largest legitimate stage-set I have ever designed. It is not only twice the area, it is twice the depth. That does not mean that every play will utilize that depth, only that it is available. The thrust stage is vast and the facilities for lighting have to be fluid. We can't afford to climb ladders after the matinee and re-angle lights for the evening production. We have what we call saturation lighting. Every area has full light in front, a side-light stage right and stage left and a back light. They cannot always be the same color and since we can't afford electronic color changers we have at least two colors for each area. Thus, for every six-by-six feet, there are four lights in the front, two in the back and one on each side. Multiply that by the total square footage of the stage and we require over three hundred spotlights. We use a couple of follow spots. Unlike the arc spots, such as are used in musicals, they are subtle incandescent lights with special equipment created for this need. The ceiling height under the beams is not tall enough to hide a bridge for electricians. We devised a little gadget with a light focused on a mirror and operated by remote control with a joy-stick such as used for steering a plane. A man in a booth at the rear of the auditorium about thirty feet from these lights moves the stick forward and the lamps tip down. When he moves the stick to the right, the beams move stage-right and so on. He also has a signal for opening and closing the iris and a handle for dimming the lights. He shares the glass booth with the stage-manager who controls the cues. This equipment is well-known in Europe. Electric companies here have had it in their catalogues for years, but no manager has ever used it. We are forced to here because we can't place men in the rafters.

Mostly the action is out on the thrust. In the more intimate productions, screens in the background close in, leaving gaps for entrances and exits. We have to clear out some of the old clichés we have been hauling about in our minds. The box set is dead, really dead, in this theatre as well as in the Vivian Beaumont Theater uptown. They are both box set proof! And that's almost better than being bomb-proof. The box set is no longer necessary in a theatre designed for the dramatization of ideas, visual ideas, not of naturalism. Naturalism would look stupid in this theatre where backgrounds may be abstract or where fragments of realism imply a setting. *After The Fall* and *But For Whom Charlie* represent two extremes. *Charlie* needs intimacy. Whatever furniture is used is expressive of the characters. It could not be picked up at a warehouse. The pieces had to be carefully chosen because the few on stage have to speak for ten other pieces which are not. The use of entrances and exits are not as stylistic as in the Arthur Miller play where there are no doors and people come out of shadowy memories of the past or the deep shadows of the present. They appear out of nothing and are picked up by lights. Even though *Charlie* is a more conventional play, it does not need the extreme naturalism of a box set. Behrman's play needs veracity rather than literal execution. Truth is not a matter of the number of square feet of wall. It is rather how true that piece is that symbolizes the wall, the quality of what is suggested by a real object or implied by an abstract element.

Designing within the physical restrictions of the open stage was familiar to David Hays. To him it gave continued stimulation rather than limitation. In addition to requiring of him further examination of the scenic relationship to the actor, repertory broke down the departmental anarchy that prevails in standard production. This tended toward closer communion among heads and a heightening of the creative experience.

Marco Millions required a little more scenery and dressing than most plays done on this kind of stage and, therefore, demanded unusual rigging where conventional methods were not available. Also, together with *After The Fall* and *But For Whom Charlie*, it faced limited storage space. Everything had to be constructed to meet both of these restrictions. We sought new ways of handling scenery because we are becoming more concerned with the vitality, the live presence of scenery as it relates to the presence of live actors. Somewhat belatedly we are coming to a point where we are not trying to compete with films and television, both of which can supply realistic backgrounds and special effects in many ways superior to those on stage. We must deal from our strength: we have the live-round person; and all aspects of the production must deal with this immediate quality, the unique quality of the live theatre which cannot be replaced by other media, no matter how good they become, how easy it is to see them, or how cheaply or handily they may be presented as mass entertainment.

I believe that most plays can be done better in this kind of theatre. The open stage for drama is an inevitable, simpler, more direct form of theatre. But we do have to seek new technical ways of mounting

"Like a giant millstone or coin turning with the world . . ." Design:
Marco Millions—*Act One: Cathay*—by David Hays. *"A continuing
group builds a relationship."*

the scenery and ways of suggesting things which will make for less and less scenery. We have to accomplish more with less or a different thing with less. We must not try to achieve the same thing with less. There is more vitality, a more direct impact, even with plays in which the stage direction specifically presupposes a proscenium.

Repertory, also, is another thing. I have worked at Stratford, Connecticut, a great deal for the New York City Ballet which is, with the Metropolitan where I have also worked, our truest repertory theatre. If the demands of repertory are not greater, they are at least different from conventional production, not in fundamental creation but in terribly important and yet secondary things: storage, re-adaptation of existing scenery, the use of rigging devices and things of that nature, the interlock and interdependence with other craftsmen working in the theatre. One can be ensnared in decisions made a month earlier after which a slight alteration in one production requires a major adaptation in the others. The O'Neill, Miller and Behrman plays were designed substantially at the same time. Jo Mielziner made every effort to get information to me the minute it was available. The relationship was enormously exciting. We knew what the others were doing, what the problems were, and we were able to discuss them and work each of them out as they arose. There is a major structure used in *After The Fall*, an elevation which we could not use in *Marco*, and it required a fair amount of engineering to remove it from the playing area. In *After The Fall* and *But For Whom Charlie*, Mr. Mielziner was able to keep it in place. In one, he used it; in the other, he masked it. He re-engineered it completely to accommodate *Marco*.

Each theatre has its own peculiarities and we are so accustomed to taking them as they come that it does not make sense to compare them with ideal situations which we don't have anywhere; nor should this theatre be contrasted with an ultimate theatre since the latter will never exist. I have not had to cope with the physical problem of this theatre except in the specific design for *Marco*. The ANTA Washington Square Theatre is by no means the plant that the Vivian Beaumont will be. Everyone is conscious of its restrictions, but the temporary stage can support a very interesting repertory of productions.

In *Marco*, we used a turn-table. It was not built-in to the theatre but was made of existing units that work for all three productions. We sliced across so that part of it could turn. It is not used to handle scenery, but to make the stage look like a giant millstone or coin turning with the world, and to give the total stage movement a circular orbital quality.

Working with a continuing group builds a relationship, a designer-director relationship such as Jo Mielziner has with Elia Kazan. I have a similar relationship with José Quintero. There is trust; and the complex mechanics of communication are made easy. This is important in any production, more so when we are working in new forms or formats. It is more than ordinary mind-reading. You must perceive another man's tentative visualizations. Our sessions together were creative and productive. I went to rehearsal every day, reviewed what didn't work and what would be needed in the coming days. We did not retire with the scripts and return with finished settings. They developed along with the plays in rehearsal. There is always a certain day after which changes cannot be made without paying a penalty. But there are numerous things that are flexible up to the end, if only in the placement of furniture and in light changes. Whatever they are, they are not annoyances or symptoms of a poor job; they are the very nature of our work, and it similarly affects directors, composers and everyone else in a community effort.

In the present theatre building, brilliant results have been achieved with the available time and money and conditions. In *Marco*, we met the theatre on those terms as well as we could; it was not actually a hardship. There are conditions in this theatre that won't have to be dealt with at the Vivian Beaumont, but they are things that can be worked around. Technically, the downtown building is not even remotely in the same class with the Vivian Beaumont. But there is excitement in a temporary building which carries you over the low spots. It is an adventure.

"This new theatre will first of all respect its audience. It hopes to reveal to them their lives."—Elia Kazan, with Arthur Miller in foreground.

The Repertory Theater's acting company assembled for the first time on October 23rd 1963. It was addressed by Robert Whitehead, Elia Kazan, Arthur Miller, José Quintero, S. N. Behrman and Harold Clurman. The final paragraphs of Mr. Kazan's speech follow.

. . . But finally, as with all things human, a theatre is known by its spirit. And I want to say something about this.

We have come together to make a theatre. We are organizing a group of human beings to try to make art, not to do business. We have not come together to sell entertainment.

This new theatre will first of all respect its audience. It hopes to reveal to them their lives. At times it will arouse them to an awareness of what is happening around us or what has happened. At other times, as a friend might, it will speak in dissension, in tones of argument. It will not always be easily digestible. But it will always be pertinent, or so we hope. That is our goal. For we believe that the theatre is not an escape from life but a part of the act of living, even a necessary part of it.

Since we are Americans, this will be an American theatre. It will be centered in New York City, but it will not be aimed at one section or group in our country. We hope it will be a world theatre, expressing the way we Americans see the world. While it will not limit itself to our time and our period, it must inevitably see things from the platform of this day. Finally, we hope, it will speak for all men by expressing what is deepest and most enduring in the lives of all men.

It will be an involved theatre, a committed theatre. It will speak for the fertile against the sterile, for inquiry and against dogma, for freedom against every enslavement, for beauty and against the frightful, for life and against death. It will not always speak with the same voice, but sometimes loud, sometimes soft and gentle, sometimes stern, sometimes laughing. For while it will try to face the truth, it doesn't feel hopeless. It is not born out of resentment, bitterness or hatred. It is here, finally, to exalt not to demean. We hope it will always speak lovingly and always without fear.

"The actor and the company are one . . ." *The interview: left to right, Arthur Miller, Robert Whitehead, Elia Kazan and a member of the Repertory Theater.*

Twenty-Five Ways
of Looking at a Company
by Sandra Hochman

WALLACE STEVENS LIVED IN TWO WORLDS: the world of real things and the world of his own imagination. He alternated between dream and reality, seeing things always as they are and things as they might be, translating the creations of sound into speech that only his exaggerated ear could hear.

In *Thirteen Ways Of Looking At A Blackbird*, Stevens examined the flight of a bird, observing how opposites could be united. He wrote:

> *A man and a woman*
> *Are one.*
> *A man and a woman and a blackbird*
> *Are one.*

He struggled toward a harmonious whole, rejecting intermediate parts, putting together the jigsaw of creature and landscape.

I had spent one day in early December at rehearsals of the Repertory Theater, speaking to the actors about the company, about their theatre and about themselves. I returned with a notebook of twenty-five ways of looking at the theatre, a dreamy notebook I had filled while speaking to them. And I kept transposing the Stevens lines in my mind, saying to myself, "The actor and the company are one."

I

The Central Plaza, near as it is to Saint Marks Place and the Saint Marks Baths, is a steam bath where the actors, walking and sitting around on benches, sweat out their lives, sweating and shedding themselves.

"My father was Sheriff Law. They used to rib us about our name. Law." It's early morning. We're leaning against the stairway on the fourth floor of the Central Plaza, once a catering establishment, now serving as a rehearsal hall. Outside on Second Avenue, everything is waking up. Upstairs in one of the ballrooms, music and pantomime have been going on for hours. The hallway is like an old casino. Young actors are getting into their scripts, holding their parts up to their faces. John Phillip Law is young, blond, slim and modest, out of California, born in Hollywood where "coyotes used to scream in our backyard." He speaks quietly. "I miss water sports. And I miss the sea. Just came back from visiting my brother in an Indian village, Yalapa, Mexico, near Puerta Vallerta. We spent a month exploring, skin diving, but it's good to be back in the theatre. You really open up when you have a chance to work with actors for a long time. In the end I'll be of more value to the theatre—and to myself." We are sitting at the foot of the staircase watching the actresses running up and down the steps. "I've worked in movies in Italy. Studied at Hawaii—psychology and mechanical engineering." We hear a piano in another room. The actor and the music seem one. "That's Quintero," he says, "rehearsing *Marco Millions*."

2

"There's more to acting than being good in one play." She turns and looks at me. Crystal Field: wild-haired, wearing blue velvet, looking like a Wallace Stevens Byzantine.

> *And then, the simpering Byzantines*
> *Fled, with a noise like tambourines.*
> *Beauty is momentary in the mind—*
> *The fitful tracing of a portal;*
> *But in the flesh it is immortal.*

"The reason I'm here? My ambition is fulfilled here. I've worked for Kazan. Played Hazel in *Splendor In The Grass*. And the leading actor in the film, *America America*—Kazan chose me to work with him to teach him how to speak English. I've been acting and dancing since childhood." Inside the larger ballroom the piano keeps repeating the same melody.

3

A bold man appears. Mad; friendly. Kindness is deep-set in his blue eyes. "I was Crystal's teacher. I've taught many of the actors in the company at my school." "I know that," I say; "and I admire you." "You do?" How pleased he is: Paul Mann jacketed in blue denim, all denim and sighs. "I've got to tell you something," he says, as if it were a secret. As if everything he says is something of secrets. "I consider being in the Lincoln Center Repertory company as simply a logical progression and, I hope, a fulfillment of all my previous theatre work. For a fact, I came to this country—I'm from Montreal—in order to become a member of a theatre company rather than to forge an individual career. I worked with the Neighborhood Playhouse, the Federal Theatre, the theatre of Erwin Piscator, New Stages and with Michael Chekhov in New York. Very important—Michael Chekhov. When I was in Russia receiving an award—I have to show you my photographs—I received the Sea Gull Medallion from the Moscow Art Theatre. They said to me, 'You studied with Chekhov?' They were awed. 'You were Chekhov's Mercutio?' Well, you know it pleased me." I think of Blake's *Inferno*, of a man swimming in fire. He's alive to everything. Puffed with the passion of a brilliant man.

4

A contrast. Reticent Faye Dunaway. "I'm new in the theatre. That's why I consider myself lucky to be here. I was born in Florida. Went to college there, and then to Boston University. I was on Broadway in *A Man For All Seasons*, with Emlyn Williams. One thing I don't like is being in the city. When I was playing in summer stock, it was wonderful in Maine by the ocean. I like water. And the country. I always wanted to be an actress."

5

Sitting in an empty room that's behind a rehearsal of *Marco Millions*. The room is eccentric: neon chandeliers; a gold mirror hangs on the wall, shiny as a fat face; wallpaper scribbled with pink flowers; dusty Venetian blinds striped red and white. The Central Plaza was built as a catering palace in the 1920's and it now sniffs of its history: a chronicle of weddings, bar mitzvahs, mystical lodge meetings, sanitation conventions, jazz concerts, rehearsals of TV sagas. I remember once seeing a sign outside the Central Plaza that read, "Marry Now—Pay Later. We Specialize In Weddings." I'm at a long table that has coffee rings worked carefully into its grain. Actors, like waiters, are banging doors as they walk in and out on their route to a dance class. Red-haired Diane Shalet passes by. "I guess you could call me a camp follower of the Repertory Theater," she says. "When I got out of Performing Arts High School, I was off to Hawaii University to be in the repertory theatre there, a really international company. We had a Chinese Julius Caesar and Japanese actors; it was marvelous. I was Barbara Allen in *Dark Of The Moon*. In school I was inspired by Angna Enters and thought I would like to create my own monologues out of poetry and paintings. I devised my own one-woman show." It seems odd: the dead room and the young girl. She's saying, "I want to give the audience something to jump out of their seats about, to give them something they might even disagree with. The theatre is a place where ideas should be bounced around. It shouldn't be a passive experience. My God, I didn't even know I thought that!"

6

Doodling: "The death of Satan was a tragedy for the imagination." An old Stevens poem. Stanley Beck—I had seen him in *The Balcony* —passes, on his way to a rehearsal. He sits for a moment in a folding chair next to the table. We talk a while about *Bee Bee Fenstermaker* and his roles on television "I'm excited," he says, "about working in a repertory theatre. Each actor has a chance to develop in this situation."

7

It's a strange situation. Talking to actors on the run from one rehearsal to another. Everyone is practicing, studying, going off in hallway corners to review lines with each other. Jack Waltzer, finished for the morning with rehearsing, sits down. "I was born in Brooklyn. Went to NYU and took business courses. I wasn't any good. I found out the theatre was the only thing that mattered to me. Later I was at the Shakespeare Festival—its second year . . ." He is nervous talking about himself. "One of the things I like about this company is getting away from type casting. Let's see, what am I interested in? I'm interested in being a better person."

8

Joined by Scott Cunningham. "There's never been anything like this in the American theatre. It's exciting and terrifying." "Terrifying in what way?" I ask. "Working with people you always admired," he says. "It's like this: I began acting when I was a kid; my big brother was interested in acting and he sort of let me tag along; once I was a self-made Dracula in a mask made from my mother's flour sack, going around spooking the neighborhood, letting out blood-curdling screams. Nobody ever found out. That was in Philadelphia. I went to Temple University. Studied fine arts as well as acting. Later, I came to New York. I walked into an off Broadway theatre and said, 'I'm an actor,' and they put me right into the play. I sculpt and paint, and I'm a make-up artist as well as an actor. Being in this company gives me a chance to play roles I wouldn't play on Broadway."

In Baudelaire's prose poem, *Vocations*, a little boy says, "Yesterday my parents took me to the theatre. In grand and sorrowful palaces, behind which you can see the sky and the sea, men and women, serious and sorrowful too . . . but much more beautiful . . . It's scary, you want to cry, and yet, somehow, it makes you feel that you, too, would like to be dressed up just like them, the actors, and do the same sort of things . . . speak with the same sort of voice."

[83]

9

"When I was at Harvard there was a group of us appearing in several plays. In fact, all of the group are still in the theatre," says Harold Scott. "We made Harvard aware of theatre. I think we were partly responsible for the new playhouse they built up there. I started acting at Exeter and won a prize in a speaking contest; wrote my own monologue which I later performed at Town Hall. By the time I got to Harvard I knew I wanted to be in the theatre. Now I'm interested in directing as well as acting. I read a great many plays. It's different reading from the directorial point of view. You don't read just for the part in it for you. When I was a kid I always knew I wanted to be an artist. Here, it's good to be working with actors you know."

10

A girl, hair color of the sun, carries a book like a missal under her arm, about to go to rehearsal of *After The Fall*. "It's the ideal theatre situation," says Mariclare Costello. "Before I came, I had done a lot of teaching. I went to Clark College, the University of Vienna—I spent a year in Austria—and got my M.A. at Catholic University of America. I like being in a company that works together in many different plays." Her face is radiant.

11

Climb the stairs to another floor. A rehearsal is breaking. Actors scatter. Suddenly I'm standing in the corner of the largest ballroom, looking at the loudspeakers on the walls, the odd assortment of things. Electric fans, motionless. A blue, huge clock on the wall. It doesn't work. Blue stars circle around the clock instead of numbers as if at the Central Plaza time is always blue, starry, celestial. Above the clock white crystal candy chandeliers. Under the clock that does not strike are screens, and fire hydrants and bars, a large bed, several crates, a victrola, a tiny table, a desk with an ashtray full of Muriel cigar boxes now Muriel-less, and a stepladder. The bed is costumed in white sheets and blankets. Even so the room seems empty. In the corner is a young actress quietly resting. Barbara Loden. I hesitate to disturb her. "Oh, that's okay. I can talk with you," she smiles. "Gadg (Elia Kazan) doesn't like us yawning or getting tired during rehearsal and insists that we rest. I came to New York from North Carolina. I never wanted to be an actress. I wanted to be something I didn't know what. I was a showgirl at the Copacabana, and a model, a Conover model. Is that place still going? I feel so far away from that world now. I started drifting into acting. If I'd been in a theatre like this sooner I would be a much better actress than I am. Working here gives you a chance to grow." Her mind brushes over some of the things that are now past.

12

Middle of the afternoon I hear the clang of the elevator merging and submerging. Lunch is over. Actors disappear through numerous doors. I sit in a folding chair on the fourth floor talking with Virginia Kaye. "The idea of a repertory theatre and the reality are different. In the beginning there's a sense of newness, the difference between thinking about it and being here, the physical aspect of 'Where do I go today?' On the fourth floor you're in the Thirteenth Century with *Marco Millions*. You take the elevator and you're in the present with *After The Fall* and Arthur Miller. I have an enormous excitement about the plays. So do my teenage sons. Outside of the theatre my main interest is my family. There are also many other things. I'm studying Italian. Tonight I'm missing a lecture on art history at the Italian American Society. I don't have time for that now. I grew up in this city . . ."

13

Would like some day to write the story of how a little boy becomes an actor. Would cast in it an actor like Michael Strong who has something of that magic lantern quality in him, a strength and boyishness in deep blue eyes and in his voice. As we talk he holds his pipe, recalling his days as a student with Gregory Peck and Efrem Zimbalist, Jr. Recently, he was in a short film directed and produced by Paul Newman, *The Harmfulness of Tobacco*. He takes out his wallet and shows me a news cutting about the film. Clipped on his wallet, the blue badge of a detective. "That's from a performance we once gave of *Detective Story* 'for detectives only.' The chief of detectives gave each cast member a badge with his initials on it and I always carry mine with me." We talk about the films he's been in and the dozens of shows in roles ranging from psychopaths to psychiatrists. We are laughing and suddenly, very seriously, we are talking again about acting. "Kazan once said to me on the phone, he said, 'I hope it can be a way of life.' That really meant something to me. I think of this company as a home. I hope it will be as wonderful as it could be."

14

He speaks in a gentle high voice, easily going from one role to another, running parts together like piano scales. ". . . And in *Camino Real*. We were in New Haven. I was handed ten dollars and told to buy a costume. I rummaged all through the town and bought some green chiffon—you remember, I wore that; also insisted on white shoes. It was right for the Baron Charlus. And one night just before going on stage, I saw a daisy sitting on a table—a prop—I picked it up and put it in my buttonhole. I got a kick later when I found out the daisy was a symbol used by Oscar Wilde. I loved that play. I hope they do it here." As David J. Stewart continues, Lepke entangles with the Baron Charlus as if each character an actor plays is one long shadow of himself. "I did a lot of research in the public library for *Murder, Inc.*, looking at pictures of the era. I found Lepke was a conservative man, soft spoken, a man of delicacy. If you saw him in an elevator on Park Avenue you would never have thought him a gangster but a business man or a banker, and that's how I played him. And you know, one of Lepke's relatives once stopped me on the street to tell me how much like him I really was." From the theatre to himself, his French wife, his two children, his work on Broadway and television, and then back to the theatre again. "I think the Repertory Theater comes the closest to giving an actor an opportunity to work as an artist in the theatre. Sometimes you're forced into clichés because of lack of time."

I5

All afternoon they rehearse *Marco Millions*. The director and the actor
tiptoe around each other in a pantomime reminiscent of children
playing a serious game. Then they start speaking in jovial hullabaloo.
For a moment the rehearsal breaks and David Wayne comes to where
I sit watching from a folding-chair perch near the door. There are just
a few minutes before rehearsal resumes. We speak swiftly. "I think
repertory is the artist's dream. It gives him a sense of belonging. Something he needs badly." We chatter like birds in a hurry. He loves to
read, to travel—Africa, Canada—to play golf. He lives in Westport;
he is an amateur carpenter and cabinet maker. And a competitive
croquet player. Although he has been in many films he prefers working in the theatre, liking musicals the best of all because "they are more
fun; the companies are larger and more diverse." He gets up quickly
and the rehearsal continues. The voice of the stage manager from
the other room recalls *The Wasteland*: "Hurry up, please; it's time."

16

I step outside. Behind me I hear a quick melody, the piano repeating
it over and over again. A conversation with Hal Holbrook weaves
in and out between the mutterings of the piano. We talk of his book,
Mark Twain Tonight, which grew out of his experiences in his show
about Twain. "I always dreamt about a repertory theatre. I got to
New York and spent ten years doing the things you have to do to
compete in the commercial theatre. I don't like being caught in a hit
for two years, and when this opportunity came to be part of a company with continuity, to do the best plays, I had to think about it. I
decided that was what I wanted and really to develop as an actor."
He relaxes in a folding-chair in the hallway, the neon chandelier shin-
ing down on a man speaking quietly. "You have to have a goal to do
your best work. The anxieties of a Las Vegas atmosphere are not good
for an actor."

Baudelaire: "Finally my soul explodes, crying, 'Anywhere!
Anywhere! Anywhere!' as long as it be out of this world."

[87]

Dashing through the corridors of the fifth floor in a plaid skirt and sweater, her hair pulled back from her face, she settles down across from me. I ask her a question. Zohra Lampert turns it around and around in her mind as if it were floating. The credulous imagination of children is in her face. She looks at me and says in a very soft voice, "I like the plays." She unwraps her lunch: some honey, cheese and crackers. "You really get a feeling of self-respect in a company like this. It doesn't interest me to be an actress in the current sense of the word. I worked with the Second City. It's funny but some of the premises used by the Second City are used by the Repertory Theater." She drips honey on a cracker. "The kind of stage, and little scenery; that sort of thing." Her voice becomes very high. Now it is floating. "I like it here. I hated dance. I didn't want to move like a *dancer*. Now I feel that I can make myself go. Because I want to."

18

Near the end of the afternoon. Time seems to have no meaning in the Central Plaza; it is so dark you can hardly tell one hour of light from another. There is no light except from the neon chandeliers. A tall blonde girl walks to the water cooler. She seems like a lion—a lion at a water cooler—and I remember La Fontaine's *A Lion In Love* "... adorned with a mane like a halo." Salome Jens turns her blonde head, sits down and talks about her life on a Wisconsin dairy farm, her titles as a girl: Miss Avalon Theatre, Miss Bay View Frolic, Miss Wisconsin Flashbulb; her beginnings in New York as a dancer studying with Martha Graham, her home in Waukesha County where her Polish mother, Salomea Szujewski, and German father, Arnold John Jens, operate a resort, *The Jolly Fisherman*; the films and plays she's been in and Salome suddenly stops. "I never dreamed of being an actress. I was interested in law and worked as a secretary one summer in a lawyer's office. I kept asking, 'What does it mean?' " The room fills with the shadows of actors reading scripts quietly together. "I'm so happy to be part of the Repertory Theater. It gives us a place where we can grow up."

[88]

19

He looks at me, answering my question. "I'm not here out of ideals. I see nothing wrong with the theatre as it exists. I mean," he smiles, "I believe in free enterprise. I'm here because I want to work with these people." Clinton Kimbrough, born in Sandusky, Ohio, one-fourth Chickasaw Indian on his mother's side, three months at the University of Oklahoma before coming to New York. He had been a corporal in the Army Signal Corps in Japan and Korea. "After being in *Our Town* I was asked to play all those parts of a hometown boy. This may seem funny, but I adore playing 'evil' more than 'good' parts. That's the direction I want to go."

20

"I like tennis even more than I like to eat, and that's a lot." Ralph Meeker, part painter, part athlete, a mixture of opposites, boyish as he smiles. We talk about the films he has been in, rumbling over his credits, running the titles together like an Odyssey of Hollywood. "I've been dying to come back to Broadway ever since *Picnic*," he says. "One of the reasons I'm here is that you won't find anyone in this group who isn't dedicated to theatre. Each person here helps the other. There are none of the jealousies you usually find." We talk about painting and music ("I wanted to be a composer."), his studies at Northwestern University, and then he says abruptly, "This role in *But For Whom Charlie* is better than anything I've ever done. Nobody in Hollywood would ever cast me in it. I play a comedy part. I really think my forte is comedy. Working with Kazan is an actor's dream. I prefer the stage to anything else. It's a marriage between the actor and the audience." His voice becomes softer as he sits back in a wooden chair. I feel as in an actor's museum. Actors passing by me on their way to work. As they might step out of a dream.

21

"My name is Joseph Wiseman. I don't want to be confused with Dr. No," he tells me confidentially. No one is listening to us. "It just happens that I'm playing an Oriental in *Marco Millions* and I don't want people to confuse the two parts. Of course," he laughs, "that's hardly

[89]

likely." What was it like to work in *Dr. No*? "Frightening. It was shot in London. They had created a replica of an atomic center that had been declassified. All those buttons. It made you realize the world could be blown up with a push of a finger. I hate to carry a gun even in the movies." The peaceful "villain," a strange mixture of scholar and actor. He speaks of everything, modestly asserted: his roles on Broadway, dozens of films and television shows, what Marianne Moore calls "a blizzard of detainments." An actor unusually mild-mannered and kind-minded, born in Canada, with "no formal theatrical training." He says, "Concerning theatre, first of all, you have to have a place to work where you are not intimidated by success."

22

"I'm a runner. What makes me run? It's a good way to work off tension. It's a tranquilizer. I run for the New York Pioneer Club. Ran in the Boston Marathon; twenty-six miles . . ." Then James Greene speaks of himself as an actor. "One thing: an actor, no matter what he tells you, is always wondering 'What am I going to be doing next?' That way, actors are never giving a hundred percent of their concentration to acting. Here, for the first time, an actor gives his complete attention to what he is doing. He's not thinking about TV or about anything else. Each actor feels, 'Now I have two years to apply myself.' " The players sit about in folding-chairs. Thousands of dinners have been served and eaten in this dining-room on the fourth floor. There is another quality to the room: quietness, as in a mansion where a secret is kept. A family secret—Was it only the play itself?—is being withheld from outsiders. "The actor is not a scavenger in this company," he continues in a subdued voice. "Here an actor can be relaxed. No thinking, 'Will it be a hit or a flop?' I'm the only actor who has been in seven of José Quintero's productions. *Girl On The Via Flaminia* is where I met my wife." The piano starts to play. A rehearsal is beginning again. José Quintero in a thick-knit yellow sweater calls the actors, hugging them and walking about as the child game starts once more. James Greene stands up. "One thing: the best thing for an actor is to be married to an actress. It's really very good; you can understand all the other's problems." He dashes away.

23

The blue reflections from the ceiling are nibbling at the walls. I've been searching all day for some answer to a never-ending question about the actor, a question in which my voice sounds like a sermon quieting a mouse in the wall. What is an actor anyway? What is he doing? The answers are still filled with knowing and not knowing. Patricia Roe loves music, seeing a few good friends, good conversation, walking, traveling, getting away from acting. "I'd like to do plays that go back to elegance and grace. The Repertory Theater is the kind of theatre I believe in, where I can stretch and develop." It's getting late. Lines from Stevens:

> You are one of the not-numberable mice
> Searching all day, all night, for the
> honeycomb.

24

"In St. Louis, the Compass Theatre, it was great. We did a new show every month. It was something like a repertory company." Barry Primus walks beside me from one floor to another. "We got invited to everybody's house. People would be really glad to see us. At first we did improvisations. Then it became a theatre and we did plays every month. We brought one to Broadway and it bombed. Coming to Broadway was an anti-climax. It was just another theatre. I enjoyed ours in St. Louis even more. Even if we had bad reviews, we had a ball. The quality of our shows was better than any of the touring shows. We got to know the actors in the road companies; they were good, but tired. Some of them had been on the road for fifteen years, and the understudies—God! the understudies never got to do anything! And they'd talk to us. We were fresh; we enjoyed what we were doing. The touring companies—they'd come to town; they'd go out and drink and—and do the same show. But the life was out of them. It made me realize a lot about the theatre. It isn't a museum. The theatre is what's taking place now; it's concerned with life, the life of this moment. At the Compass, we did one show after another, but they weren't connected. A show has to have a 'line' to it. It has to have a reason for being done, here at the Repertory Theater. All these plays have something to say about the present. They have something to say about our world now. They have . . . a 'line.' "

25

I remember *The Theatre and Its Double* in which Antoine Artaud wrote that a poet should be someone set on fire, and his words should beckon from the flames. This is true of an actor.

It is evening. Jason Robards, Jr., has been pacing all day within the white tape-markings of the rehearsal hall, a tiger in a cage. To anyone who has never seen this zooish man come alive on stage—there is a trapped animal quality to him—Jason Robards stays in the mind as a very great tiger who knows what he is growling. Rehearsing, there is a master control in his body, in his voice. An energy, if let loose, would blow up the Central Plaza. "Hello." After the five-hour rehearsal, Jason is smiling. We descend to the street-floor restaurant for a bite. Upstairs, Jason is just another member of a company. But in the restaurant, the waiters dance around like mountebanks, performing somersaults to please. Never does a bowl of matzoh-ball soup arrive so quickly. "I needed a break from that Broadway routine," Jason says. "Here, there's a new form in the play. An actor's able to do the kind of things he always wanted to do." He has just enough time to finish his soup and run back upstairs.

I'm outside. Night. It's raining the terrible first rain of early December. No boots. No borrowed umbrella. "Would you like a lift?" An older man standing under the awning turns to me. "Don't be afraid of me. I saw you talking to Jason Robards. I'd be glad to help out anyone who was sitting with him." "That's alright, but I think I'll walk." It's late. I had missed the chance to ask Jason about his life in Chicago, his impressions of his father—so many things. Second Avenue is cold and wet. I'm thinking of the actors who told me something of their lives, of the company and what it means to them. "The imagination leads and the deed follows," one actor had said. I think of verse by Stevens.

> *We do not say ourselves like that in poems.*
> *We say ourselves in syllables that rise*
> *From the floor, rising in speech we do not speak.*

Harold Clurman

Director; theater critic, *The Nation*; author, *The Fervent Years, Lies Like Truth*; co-founder and managing director, Group Theatre; Chevalier, Legion of Honor; Honorary L.L.D., Bard College; Honorary D.F.A., Carnegie Institute of Technology; Executive Consultant, Repertory Theater of Lincoln Center.

Arthur and Barbara Gelb

Husband and wife writer-team; authors of *O'Neill*, his first complete biography. Mr. Gelb is staff member of the *New York Times*, formerly assistant director of Cultural News and currently assistant Metropolitan editor.

Alfred Harbage

Author of *Shakespeare's Audience, Theatre For Shakespeare, As They Like It: A Study of Shakespeare's Moral Artistry, Shakespeare and The Rival Traditions, Cavalier Drama*; Cabot Professor of English Literature, Harvard University; Honorary L.L.D., University of Pennsylvania; Scholarship Award, American Shakespeare Festival and Academy.

Sandra Hochman

Voyage Home, first volume of verse, published in Paris, 1960; *Manhattan Pastures*, Yale Younger Poets Award, second volume published 1963; *Poems in Print*, bi-monthly program on WBAI.

Barry Hyams

Director, Public Relations, Repertory Theater of Lincoln Center; theater critic, *American Examiner*; producer, *Ulysses in Nighttown*; director, Foo Hsing Opera.

John Simon

Author, critical essays, *Acid Test*; drama critic, *Hudson Review*; film critic, *New Leader*; taught literature at Harvard University, Bard College, University of Michigan and Massachusetts Institute of Technology.

Book design by Quentin Fiore

*All photos except the O'Neill snapshot and
the two stage designs are by Inge Morath.*

Sketches by Judy Nathanson

Printed by Clarke & Way, Inc.